Dancing with Angels

Jane Hart

PublishAmerica

Baltimore

ISBN: 1-59129-448-7
PUBLISHED BY PUBLISHAMERICA BOOK
PUBLISHERS
www.publishamerica.com
Baltimore

Printed in the United States of America

Dedication

For my husband,
Bill,
who cooked, cleaned and spent many long hours alone
while I stayed to myself working on my first endeavor.
He believed in me and he missed me.

Acknowledgments

To my sisters,
Marty and Erma,
who helped me put my story together.
And to all my friends who encouraged me to write this book.

CHAPTER 1

"When will this day ever end?" she says to herself. Her dress is sticking to her body, perspiration is running down her face and between her breasts, her hair is damp and dusty and the salty perspiration is making her eyes burn. The weather has been unpredictable for the past few weeks. One day is chilly, the next warm. In the past few weeks it seemed to rain more often than compared to a month ago. It reminds her of the changing of seasons. "Maybe it's spring, but it sure does feel like summer." She talks to herself often. It helps pass the time while she travels with the soldiers. "I hope the troops soon stop to rest." It's been hours since she's had food or water. She's hot and sticky, hungry and thirsty, tired and dirty. And to top all that off, clouds are rolling in; it looks like a storm is coming. She had never been afraid of summer storms before, but since the battle of Atlanta and because she now travels with fighting troops, the sound of thunder reminds her of gunfire, and each bolt of lightening brings back memories of the fires in the fields. She has journeyed in rain, snow, and, at times, knee-deep mud since leaving Atlanta after the battle of 1863. "How long have I been following the troops?" she asks herself. "If I could remember the passing of one season to the next, it might help determine how long it's been." But she can't remember if there had been more than one winter.

The year is 1865. A brigade of Rebel soldiers is traveling north from Atlanta. Florence, a young female slave, is traveling with them. Florence is very petite—maybe not even five feet tall—and for every step the soldiers take, she has to take two. Her cheekbones are high. Her brown eyes are large and round with eyelashes so long that they tickle her eyebrows. When she smiles, she reveals perfectly white teeth. She considers her smile to be her best feature and feels lucky to have never suffered a toothache. Her hair is long and smooth and tied back with a piece of rope. Because she is what some call a half-breed, her characteristics are varied and her skin color is a beautiful, radiant light brown. Her only dress is faded and tattered. She travels barefoot. When she has the opportunity to bathe, she does so in nearby streams or rivers. She washes her dress and puts it back on wet. During the cold of last winter, Florence performed the difficult mission of stealing a coat and boots from a dead soldier. She carries them with her. They helped her keep warm when it was cold but right now, the days are warm, and a coat and boots are extremely burdensome to have to drag with her. She has no choice. She will need the protection when winter sets in.

She will never forget Atlanta, or the sadness she felt on the day she left. She was only seventeen. Since then, she has suffered through cold and hunger, witnessed many battles, watched soldiers die and has spent the last year or so alone and afraid.

Florence was given her name by a slave nanny when she was taken from her mother at birth. She was born in a shack, taken from her mother and nursed by a nanny. Of course, she doesn't remember life before the age of five or six, but she does remember this is what always happened to newborn baby slaves. She doesn't know much about her mother, except she surmised that her mother must have been very pretty. While working in the fields and listening to the other women talk, she learned that her mother was a Negro slave and her father was white. The women in the fields told her that her father was either one of the bosses or the master of the plantation. They said that a boss, or the master, often came to the slaves' shacks during the night to look for a young, attractive Negro female. It wasn't always the same man, but whoever he was, they all performed in the same manner. He would force the girl of his choice into a wagon and take her to a place away from the plantation and use her for sex. On their return, the girls all told the same story. The man always covered his face with a handkerchief so he couldn't be recognized, took her far away, pushed her to the ground, spread her legs and forced himself into her long and hard. If she tried to get away or scream, the man would slap and kick her so badly that she would be nearly unconscious. But he would take her anyway, while her cuts and bruises bled on his white shirt. When he was finished with her, the man would leave her there in the dark. If she didn't find her way back in time to be working the fields at dawn, a search party was sent out and when she was found, she was whipped and drug back to the shanny. By this time the other women were already working in the fields, so she would be left with her hands and feet still tied from the same rope used to drag her. She would be left lying in the dirt to bleed and bake in the sun until late in the day when the others returned to rescue her. The women told Florence that her mother was one of the prettiest, so she was often taken away in the wagon late at night.

CHAPTER 2

Florence does a lot of reminiscing while on long marches with the troops. Today is no exception. The march is longer than usual, the heat is intense, her sweaty body is streaked with dust, and the soles of her feet, even though they're tougher than shoe leather, are burning. She wonders if this is the way it feels to walk on hot ashes. To lessen the discomfort of the moment, she allows her thoughts to drift back on how she got herself into this predicament in the first place. Florence thought back to the day the Yankee soldiers stormed into Atlanta. She remembers it as though it was yesterday. "It had to be more than a year ago," she says to herself.

She remembered it was December, 1863. The Yankees seemed to come from nowhere. Within minutes, their presence was know throughout the city as well as to the outlying plantation owners. They arrived on horseback, hollering and laughing. They were swinging their swords over their heads while firing gunshots so loud that the ground rumbled. They acted like crazy men. They instantly set fire to the cotton fields as though it was the first and most important mission they had to accomplish. Florence can still envision the fields burning for as far as the eye could see. It was like looking at an ocean of red-hot flames, but without the water. The waves of fire burned hard and fast. There was fire everywhere. The Yankees went from field to field, dwelling to dwelling and barn to barn with their torches. She watched her owner's house and outbuildings burn to the ground. She can still hear the horrifying sounds coming from the livestock as they tried to escape the flames. The animals that did escape were running around confused and lost. She remembers the Yankees entering the city and destroying the cemetery. "Those crazy men took such pleasure in crushing the monuments," she said to herself. They rode their horses high and fast and hollered like a team of barbaric maniacs. They broke off the marble lambs and the miniature guardian angel statues from the graves of little children. She watched in disbelief while those "barbaric crazy men" dug up graves and stole the silver name plates from coffins. She watched them remove the dead from the graves and mausoleums so they could reuse the openings to bury their own. She doesn't remember how many days the battle lasted. She does remember days turning into nights and nights into days and how she hid and ran from one place to another to avoid being caught by those "damned Yankees."

Suddenly, and as though they were on a bigger and better mission, the crazy men stormed out of Atlanta almost as fast as they had stormed in. Behind them, they left the city in total destruction. Fragments of wagon wheels, animal carcasses and dead bodies were strewn everywhere. Within hours, bushwhackers, robbers and deserters arrived to rummage through the ruins. Scavengers fought between themselves and even killed each other over a pair of silver candlesticks or a piece of jewelry. There seemed to be no end to the destruction.

She looks back now at how some of the plantation owners had lost almost everything: their livestock, out buildings, crops, and in many cases, their homes. She is saddened by their losses but considers them to be more lucky than the slaves. The owners still have their family and they didn't lose their land. They had neighbors and relatives offering them a place to stay and food to eat. They put their pride aside, slept in someone else's bed, and ate their neighbor's food. They had their land and most had the resources to rebuild and start over. But us slaves, she thinks, we had no place to go. We had to keep running and hiding in the ruins. Most of us didn't know if we would be beaten or killed if found roaming the streets. If not killed for roaming, they knew for sure that they would be blamed with the stealing. It would be taken for granted that the Negros should be held responsible for the scavenging, the killing and any other destruction that could not be charged to the Yankees. The slaves rumored among themselves and arrived at all sorts of conclusions as to why they thought they would be dead one way or the other in the end. With this way of thinking and with all the rumors, the slaves had convinced themselves that they would not survive the aftermath of the Yankee invasion. Florence wondered how many stayed and what had happened to them.

Florence remembers that slaves were not permitted to stay together as families. They were either taken from their mother at birth, separated at slave auctions, or traded with other land owners. Sometimes, while working the fields, she recalls seeing wagons pull away with the elderly, the sick or the very young. She knew they were off to auction or trade, and assumed that the sick were either hanged or shot. Later in the day, she would see the same wagon return with bigger and stronger workers. They were transported like cattle, she thought to herself. She wondered if any of the women she saw on the wagons was her mother.

Florence decided to clear her mind and think of more pleasing thoughts to help pass the time. She would change her thinking to the good things she remembers about Atlanta. She reminded herself of the elegance of the plantation. The main house was breathtaking, so huge and so white. The windows went from floor to ceiling and she could see the beauty of the floral drapes, tied back with fancy hooks and bows. She imagined the interior filled with the finest china, furniture, imported rugs, fancy mirrors and even a grand piano. The front and sides of the structure had enormous white pillars surrounding a most magnificent wrap-a-round porch. She thought of the times she had hidden in the bushes to watch Sunday dinner being served on the porch. After each meal, the men would gather off to one side to smoke pipes and cigars and to talk, probably about business or the female slaves. The women sat on wicker rockers giggling and gossiping over a cup of tea or coffee. She remembers hearing the children laugh and watching them play in the perfectly landscaped yard. They usually played hide and seek. The game always created a chance that Florence would be discovered while hiding behind the trees and bushes. Of course, she never was, but the thought always brought excitement to her and made her feel as though she was one of the children playing the game. The landscaping was flawless. Depending on the time of the year, different flowers and shrubs of the season were in full bloom. Flowering plants hung from hooks on the porch, creating a cascade of color all around the big house. The workers who were considered to be gardeners, worked from sunup to sundown. Florence remembers seeing the gardeners, on hands and knees, digging any weed or dandelion they found in the grass. Of course, if the dandelion was dug before it bloomed, the plant was taken back to the shanny and cooked with the next meal. Florence remembers the bitter taste of dandelion and has decided that she doesn't miss it. The weed free grass was always green and soft, and looked so inviting. She planned to take a sneak across that flawless lawn on her bare feet one night. She could only imagine the freshness and softness compared to the pricking of the weeds and the cracking of the dry red clay she felt under her feet while working the fields. Even though she hated the fields, Florence loved the plantation and hoped to one day become a servant and work in the main house. She dreamed about serving the Sunday meal on the porch. After dinner, she would serve coffee to the men while they puffed on pipes and cigars. While she served tea and dessert to the women, maybe she might have the chance to overhear the latest gossip and finally learn what they had so much to giggle about.

She finds herself again thinking of the heartache. She cannot clear her mind of her mother and wonders if she is dead. "If so, at least she is in peace." Florence thinks back at how and why she made the quick decision to leave Atlanta. After the battle, she heard that some slaves wasted no time in joining up with the Rebel soldiers. They planned to travel as far north as Virginia in hopes of finding work. She thought of those who were forced to stay behind because they were too old and unable to venture. "Did they starve to death or were they killed?" she asks herself. Florence knew she had to leave, and soon; she couldn't wait until she got caught or became too weak to travel.

Florence was sure that a young attractive Negro woman like herself could find work up north. Her decision to go had been quick and easy. She would sneak off behind Rebel troops and stay far enough behind so she wouldn't be noticed. She knew that the Negro men who joined the troops would become soldiers if they were willing to fight, but she didn't know how or if a Negro woman would be welcomed. She would have to sneak and hide and plan that when the troops broke camp, she would eat the scraps left behind and hide in nearby woods or under any bush she could find to sleep. Without a second thought, Florence followed the first brigade of Rebel troops that marched north out of Atlanta.

Sometimes they marched for days without food or rest on the roughest roads she had ever seen. Sometimes they marched in snow or mud up to their ankles. The weather was cold and wet. She was miserable. Many nights were so cold that Florence worried she might freeze to death. She occasionally questioned her decision to leave Atlanta. Maybe if she had stayed, she might have found a way to survive. But the cold and hunger was not the most devastating part of her adventure. Most horrifying to her were the murderous battles she had witnessed and the battles she knew were yet to come. She learned that when the soldiers slept on the roads using their weapons like pillows, and when they kept their ammunition close at hand, she could expect that at the break of dawn there would be another battle. When Florence suspected a battle, she searched for a hiding place and waited for the sounds of gunfire to begin. Some battles were ferocious and lasted for hours. Some battles were quick and over in minutes. But always, after any battle, when the gunfire ended, she could hear the screams and the cries of death until each departing soldier took his last breath. If soldiers were injured but could not be rescued, the troops moved on without them. The sounds from the moaning were left behind only to be eliminated slowly from earshot by distance.

CHAPTER 3

The battle of September 17, 1864, was one of the worst she
had seen. The night before, the troops slept on their arms along
the road. As she expected, the fighting began just after dawn.
They were somewhere in Maryland, and the troops had orders
to take a bridge. The bridge had a beautiful arc shape. It was
built of mountain stone with each stone appearing to be carefully
placed individually so that not a stone would be too big, or too
small, for the one next to it. The bridge wasn't very long. It
covered a tiny stream and was surrounded by high banks and
dirt roads coming from three different directions. It was
protected by huge shade trees. She had never seen a more
breathtaking sight. She hoped the battle would not end with
this beautiful setting being scarred forever by the blood of war.

Fighting for the bridge went on for most of the day. The
Rebels returned Yankee fire until they had only a few rounds of
ammunition left, but they continued their advance until they
shot all their cartridges away. When the ammunition was gone,
they hid in trenches on a small hill leading to the bridge and
stood their ground until dark, when the firing ceased. The next
morning, before dawn, a supply wagon came and replenished
the troops with more ammunition. They were given orders to
hold their ground at all costs and told that reinforcements were
on the way. The same morning, September 18, 1864, the Rebels
were forced to retreat back to the foot of the hill and began to
fight all over again. It seemed like yesterday had never

happened. The shooting was fierce, and soldiers on both sides were collapsing like positioned targets. Florence had never seen so many dead and wounded. The ground around the bridge was covered with soldiers, some on top of the other and not one of them moving. The cannons were so loud that Florence covered her ears while she sat in hiding. She could still feel the ground rumble with each cannon fired. The reinforcements never came. The Yankees held the hill all day. At about five o'clock in the evening, the shooting stopped. The Rebels could not take the hill or advance to the bridge. They suffered very heavy losses. They lost all their belongings. Even their knapsacks with letters and pictures from home were burned. Everything they owned was destroyed. They didn't have a change of clothing, not a bite of food or a drop of water. All they had was the dirty, torn, blood-stained clothes they had worn to fight yesterday's battle. The next two days were spent bringing in the dead and wounded. Florence would never understand the importance of taking such a small area at the expense of so many human lives. It was rumored that the Yankees were rewarded with whiskey for taking the bridge and spent the next two days in a drunken stupor.

Three days after the battle, wagons arrived to refurnish ammunition, a limited supply of clothing, food and medical supplies. Once the supplies were off-loaded and the wagons were empty, they used the same wagons to load the dead and wounded. The new supply of ammunition seemed more satisfying to the troops than shoes and blankets. With fresh food and clothing, the troops were recuperated and ready to move on with momentum. Florence wondered about their dedication.

CHAPTER 4

While revisiting all that has happened, Florence is able to propose some idea of the length of time she had been traveling. The first few months of travel had been during the second half of the winter of 1863, just after the Battle of Atlanta. She remembers the bitter cold and how she could see her breath in the air. "I was so cold, I wonder how I ever survived," she said to herself. For the first time in her seventeen years, she saw snow fall. Florence thought the flakes were fascinating. She was amazed at the different sizes and shapes of each flake and how light they felt when she caught them in her open hands. They always melted instantly, leaving her with cold, wet hands. Florence also discovered that snow created slippery and difficult walking conditions. And as the snow melted, the mud got deeper. Florence wasn't sure she liked snow.

She remembered how scared she was when she stole the coat and boots from the dead soldier to protect herself from the cold. She remembers having to step over dead bodies before finding a coat that wasn't saturated in blood. She doesn't remember how she got the boots. Florence still worries that God will punish her for stealing. She prays every day for forgiveness. She remembered that the biggest battle, the battle for the bridge, had taken place in September, 1864. In the spring and summer that followed, she remembers the fresh fruits and the soothing warm sun. Putting her thoughts together, she realizes that when the upcoming warmer season passes, she will be faced with the beginning of her second winter on the road. If she stays until winter, she is sure it will become the turn of the sixth season since she has been traveling with the troops. "I will never make it through another winter," she said to herself. During most of the time, in the past year and a half, the weather was unfavorable. If she wasn't wet and cold, she was hot and sweaty. If the temperature was pleasant, the roads were either very dusty or very muddy. She was constantly hungry, thirsty, dirty and tired. Today is no exception. She can't remember a perfect traveling day.

Florence is tired of the hunger, the cold, and the dirt. She has decided that she has gone far enough. She hopes to be far enough north that she would no longer be considered a slave. Back in Atlanta, while working in the fields, she had learned that northern people don't believe in slavery. "The farther north, the less chance of wandering into a slave town; on the other hand, the farther north, the harder the winters," she thinks out loud. She has made up her mind to find a place to settle before winter sets in. While traveling, she has been close to or walked around many towns and small villages. But she never had enough faith in herself to leave the security of the troops. She never knew where she was and hesitated to wander into an unknown village or town in Someplace U.S.A. She worried about finding work, food, and most of all, a place to live. The troops often talk about going home when the war is over. Florence wonders where home is for these men. She hopes and prays for the war to stop. "But what will happen to me, then? I'm eighteen now, old enough to fend for myself. I must find a place to settle and find work."

Looking back, Florence remembers some of the fearful times she had encountered while on the road with the troops. One memory in particular that comes to mind is the time when, on a perfectly beautiful morning, and after an unusually good night's sleep, she had let her guard down. Because she was feeling very relaxed and unhurried, she lingered over her meal much longer than usual. She was discovered by a soldier who returned to camp in search of something he had left behind. She remembered that the days had been warm, and the soldiers were finding fresh berries, squirrel, venison, rabbit, fish, and sometimes a pheasant or two. They had an ample supply of food and left more scraps than usual. She was hungry and was enjoying her feast in such a restful daydreaming state that she allowed the soldier to sneak up on her. There was a quick glance between the two, but no words were spoken. Her casual, relaxing morning had within a few seconds intensified from daydreaming to nightmare. Florence was very frightened and sure the soldier would report his findings to his superior. She worried that the troops would chase her off, or even worse, capture her and maybe even rape her like she had seen so often in Atlanta. As the days passed, nothing Florence had imagined happened. She became confident that the soldier said nothing of his discovery. A few weeks later, and on another beautiful, warm spring morning, she stopped at a nearby stream to splash dust from her face. Again she allowed herself too much casual time and was spotted by another soldier. No words were uttered, but an affectionate glace took place between the two that seemed to last forever. Florence has been traveling with these men for more than a year now, and suddenly she realized that most likely they knew all along she had been following. She decided that they had no plans to harm her. She felt relieved and decided that she would no longer have to continue the unnecessary burden of hiding and sneaking. She still remains cautiously behind while traveling and never joins them while camping, unless invited. She continues to eat from abandoned campsites.

Now that she camps within an earshot of conversation, she has, on occasion, overheard the troops talk about their families. Especially their mothers and girlfriends. Florence liked to be close by when the mail wagon caught up with the soldiers. She enjoyed watching the excitement around camp when the men received letters and packages from home. Socks and gloves are the most popular items sent from mothers. They also received an abundant amount of writing tablets and pencils. Florence thought that families sent writing supplies to encourage the soldiers to write a letter home. Once in a while they got foodstuffs like cookies or homemade candy. Such items never survived the trip.

Once while she sat within hearing distance, she overheard the troops talking kindly of her. The troops and Florence have never had conversation. They never asked her where she came from; they didn't even ask her name. And of course, Florence remained quiet and never offered information. So when talking among themselves, the troops always referred to her as "the Negro lady." Yesterday when she heard them talking, one soldier commented about how amazed he was at the "Negro lady's" motivation and determination. Some of the troops talked about her pleasant appearance and her small stature. They all agreed that she is clean and keeps herself as presentable as possible under the circumstances. They discussed her courage and decided that someone with so much incentive and determination should no longer be called "the Negro lady." Instead of asking Florence for her name, they decided to name her themselves. They wanted something appropriate for such a "special lady." They agreed that she has proven to be strong and reliable, and a woman with that kind of backbone should have a strong and yet graceful feminine name. With only a few nominations, they easily settled on Mary, a name they thought meant strong, and

Elizabeth, which they agreed sounded graceful. From now on, they will call her Mary Elizabeth. Florence liked her new name and decided that hereafter she will be known as Mary Elizabeth.

CHAPTER 5

The soldiers continue to move, the day is getting warmer and dust is everywhere. Dirt and grime is in her hair, in her eyes and she can even feel the grit in her teeth. Her dress is almost brown from the soot, and the perspiration running down her back is so heavy that she imagines streaks of mud. "It must be late in the afternoon," she mumbles to herself. The storm is becoming more threatening. She can hear thunder and see lightening at a distance. She's getting more anxious to stop and take shelter. "Finally, oh, thank you, God," she said. The soldiers finally stopped! Mary Elizabeth sat under a shade tree rubbing her sore feet. She blotted perspiration from her face and neck with leaves that had fallen to the ground. She can't wait to bathe. She remained at a comfortable distance to watch for the next movements of the troops. She could always tell from their activities if this was going to be a short stop or an overnight rest. Within minutes she could see their tents being staked. Medical supplies and food were taken from the wagon, and she noticed they didn't seem to be concerned with the ammunition. This is a good sign, Mary Elizabeth thought to herself. The soldiers prepared an area for cooking and posted their colors. She had never seen camp set up like this before. It looked like a little town, with two rows of white tents spaced evenly and furnished with a cot and a backless folding chair. The troops casually began going through their personal belongings. Some began writing in ledgers, and some read letters from home. Others wandered to the nearby stream and began washing their clothes. They hung ropes from tent to tent and draped their wet clothing over the ropes to dry. It reminded her of the ropes that hung from shanny to shanny back in Atlanta. Mary Elizabeth had never seen the soldiers this relaxed before. "I wonder where we are?" she says out loud to herself. "It sure is beautiful and peaceful." She has always had the tendency to appreciate new scenery, and since leaving Atlanta, she thought on more than one occasion that she had discovered the most beautiful place on earth. But this place is the best of all, she thought to herself. She can see rolling hills for miles in all directions. Even the storm clouds that are rolling in add a beautiful purplish color to the backdrop of her view. There are hundreds, maybe thousands, of trees and a small crystal clear stream that added the finishing touch to this perfect setting.

Even though Mary Elizabeth followed the soldiers at a modest distance, she knows that when they set up camp, sometimes one of them will seek her out and invite her to his tent. He will share his bed in exchange for food and drink. She is sure that tonight she will have shelter from the storm and something to eat without having to scavenge. She admits to herself that sometimes even the sex is pleasing.

William is about six feet tall, very blond and looks as though he is too young to shave. He is very thin, but so are most of the soldiers. She guessed he is not more than eighteen. When he talks, his voice sometimes changes from high to low and his face turns red. Mary Elizabeth can tell he is embarrassed. When William makes his invitation, he never approaches her. Instead, he stares at her until he catches her attention, then he smiles and winks. This evening, Mary Elizabeth returned the friendly wink and quickly searched for a secluded place to bathe.

A night with William is always pleasurable. He likes to

fondle and always takes his time to prepare her for his entry. He would slowly bathe using water from a basin while she watched. Tenderly, he always ask her to slowly and gently wash his back. His slow, inviting actions and her gentle washing and rinsing often led to a whole-body bath for William. He unselfishly set the pace, leaving her feeling appreciated and wanted. William's affection and kindness always added to her intense excitement. She felt respect from William. Without exception, he was careful to withdraw at just the right time. Some of the other troops were not kind and never offered affection. They were dirty, very forceful and quick. She would have to threaten to bite or kick to persuade them to withdraw. She didn't want to be with child and had learned, from William, that a man must withdraw just before he is ready to plant his seed. "It's the only way to be sure I don't leave you with child," William said.

CHAPTER 6

Mary Elizabeth didn't leave William's tent until dawn. She found a secluded spot to bathe and then sat high on some rocks and watched the sun rise. Again, she studied the perfect view. Last night's storm had been mild. Now the skies are blue and clear, and the air is clean and warm. Thinking that yesterday's march was all uphill, Mary Elizabeth presumed they must be on top of a mountain. At a distance, she could see what resembles another mountain. It was directly across from where the troops set up camp. She then looked at the downward side of the mountain from which she is sitting. She looked over tree tops with green leaves so bountiful that it looked as though she could walk across the tops of them. The valley between the two mountains was green and plush. In the valley, she could see the sun shimmering off small lakes and water ways. It was gorgeous; she knew this was a sight she would never forget.

For the first time since leaving Atlanta, Mary Elizabeth wasn't hungry. Instead of eating, she wandered closer to camp, hoping to overhear conversation from the troops. She was interested in finding out where they are. The men were casually sitting around the cooking area eating bacon and bread. The coffee smelled good. She wished she could have a cup. She heard them saying that they were approaching a small town in Pennsylvania. Their captain told them that they were to scout the area and wait for orders. They planned to be here a couple of days or maybe even a week. With that news, she knew she had time to venture. So she set out on a leisurely stroll.

Mary Elizabeth walked up stream, out of the sight of camp, and took another warm bath. She felt refreshed and ready to explore. "I will follow the stream so I don't get lost," she mumbled to herself. The water was only knee deep and as clear as the morning air. The flow was gentle and calm and traveled at an even rate. It rippled over slime-covered rocks and a very healthy-looking green moss. Occasionally, she could see small rainbow trout. She knew they were rainbow because when the sun shone on them they gave off a glow of pretty blues, pinks and greens. Another thing she had learned from the troops when they talked about home and their fishing stories. The beautiful surroundings, the soothing sounds, and the fresh clean smell gave her the feeling that she was in paradise. "I wonder if this is what it's like to be in heaven?" she ask herself. Thinking back over the last year, with the war, the cold and the hunger, Mary Elizabeth remembers times when she wished she could die and pass on. She believes that the way life is for her, the troops and the slaves, as they are living it now, would surely credit them for time spent in hell. She figured that anyone who lives on earth in this time of war and bitterness is living a pure life of hell. She believes that when a human being passes on, there are no choices to be made between God and the devil. "The devil has us now and God is waiting his turn. Life is hell, death is heaven," she said out loud. With this idea, she was sure that her mother had spent her time in hell and is now resting in heaven. Mary Elizabeth is sure that someday she will connect with her mother and they will share a new and better life together in heaven.

After stopping several times to splash the fresh, cool water on her face and spin around barefoot in the soft green grass, she allowed her mind to clear. She didn't want to have anything to think about. She only wanted to listen to the quietness. She lay on the cool, soft grass and looked into the clear sky. "Can I hear quiet?" she asked. After lying there, in silence, for a few minutes, she became bored. She jumped up and decided she wanted to pretend that she was dancing. Remembering some of the hymns the workers used to sing while picking cotton in the fields back in Atlanta, she began to sing. She jumped in the air to the tune of Amazing Grace. "A-maaa-zz-i-nn-g G-r-AAA-c-e," long slow spin, "how sweet the thought," slow bend at the waist, "or is it how sweet it is?" She couldn't remember. It didn't matter; she would hum the rest. She jumped as high and as graceful as she could. She danced slow spins and long, low bends while swirling her arms high into the air. She spun so fast that she became dizzy and fell to the ground. She laughed and danced with a happy heart. She made believe that she was dancing with angels. The angels have long, white gowns that flow when they move. They have long, blond, curly hair and carry white daises. They are barefoot, the same as Mary Elizabeth. Mary Elizabeth's angels move like butterflies; they are so graceful they seem to float in mid-air. Mary Elizabeth and the angels hummed and danced until their legs were so tired that suddenly they all fell to the ground. They lay flat on their backs in a circle, holding hands while staring up at the clear blue sky. They lay there giggling and humming until Mary Elizabeth forced herself to return to reality. She wanted to stay with the angels longer but knew she had to start moving again. "Should I go forward or turn around and start back to camp?"

Mary Elizabeth tried to avoid thinking about turning back. She felt as though she had someplace special to be today. "Maybe it's a message from God; maybe He sent the message to me by way of the angels. I must make a decision; which way do I want to go?" She knew the walk back up hill would take more time than it took to come down, but it was probably only late morning and it would be hours before dark. She is on level ground, walking forward would be easy, and the notion of turning back would ruin her perfect day. She couldn't dismiss the unexplainable intense feeling she is going through. Something, or someone, is telling her that today is special. "I must go forward, just a little farther," she said.

After rounding another bend in the stream, and not far in front of her, she could see what appeared to be a railroad track. She was curious and knew she had to investigate. "I will explore the tracks for just a short distance, then follow the tracks back to the stream. That way I won't get lost," Mary Elizabeth said to herself. She had only gone a short stretch and just within her view, she could see large buildings set off by a skyline of mountains in the background. It looks like the railroad tracks lead directly to the structures. "It looks like a town!" she says. "This must be the small town in Pennsylvania that I heard the men talking about this morning." It looks to her that this town sits in the valley that she was overlooking earlier in the day. She could turn around and see the mountain she had just walked, and in front of her, at a distance, she could see the trees of the other mountain. She is excited. "There will be no turning back. I will go farther. Maybe this will be my new home. This is my perfect day. Thank you, angels," she said to herself.

Discreet and unsure of herself, Mary Elizabeth approached what looks like a main street. She doesn't want to be noticed, so she remains close to the buildings and quietly makes her way. Soon she is in what looks like the center of a very small town. To her right is the most beautiful stone church she has ever seen. It is surrounded by a thick, black iron fence. The fence doesn't look like it was intended to keep people out. It is only maybe two feet high and has a wide top railing. The rail offers an inviting place for people to sit, and by the looks of things, it serves its purpose. The people sitting on the rail were casually talking among themselves and didn't seem to notice her arrival.

Across the street was another church. The brick was painted white and the trim around the windows was painted black. The church has a very high, pointed steeple, and in the middle of the steeple is a huge black bell. On the other side of the four corners is a very large red brick building with big round pillars on its porch. She can see a clock tower on the roof but couldn't see what time it is. "That building looks official," she said, but couldn't decide what it was. On the fourth corner was a pack of horses and empty wagons. The trees along the streets are in full bloom with flowering buds. The sidewalks are brick and the railroad tracks run right down the middle of the cobble street. When she took a second glance at the horses and wagons, Mary Elizabeth suddenly felt fear. The wagons reminded her of the slave wagons she had seen so many times in Atlanta. She hoped she hadn't wondered upon a slave auction. "Am I far enough north?" she ask herself.

Mary Elizabeth is beginning to feel nervous and afraid. She stood perfectly still, remained close to the buildings and listened for the sounds of a slave auction. She carefully peeked round the corner from the large red brick building and could see a crowd of people. She began to feel like a fugitive who is about to be caught. However, she did not see a slave platform like to ones used in Atlanta to display and auction slaves. She had heard that a slave for sale was usually stripped naked before being put on display. The crowd usually reacted with applause, booing or laughter. Realizing she wasn't hearing those kinds of sounds, and the people were not crowded around any one display, she began to relax. After a longer second peek, she noticed the people were casually wondering around and most were carrying shopping baskets. She saw fresh vegetables, eggs, meats and even fresh-cut flowers on display tables. "It looks like a market," she said to herself. She slowly merged in with the shoppers; she was very nervous, and also very curious. The shoppers were handing coins and paper in exchange for the produce. She had to assume it was money, although she had never seen any.

A kindly-looking white gentleman says, "Afternoon."

She replies, "Good afternoon, sir.

"Seems like a friendly place," she mumbles. "It doesn't seem to matter that I'm Negro." She hadn't eaten all day and now she is hungry. The food looks awfully inviting but she knew not to steal. When Mary Elizabeth noticed a Negro woman carrying a basket, her only thought was that this woman must be a servant doing her master's shopping. She approached the Negro woman carrying the shopping basket and said: "Afternoon."

The woman replied: "Good afternoon, are you enjoying the market?"

"Oh yes, it's nice."

The woman extended her hand and said: "I'm Carrie Thompson."

"I'm Mary Elizabeth."

"Never saw you before; are you new in town?"

"Just visiting."

"How long will you be staying?"

"I'm not sure. I'm looking for work; if I find something here, I might stay for a long time."

Mary Elizabeth likes the looks of the town, and she likes Carrie too.

"Who do you work for, Carrie?" she asked.

"I work for myself."

Carrie went on to explain that she works for different families: doctors, lawyers etc. She goes to their houses and does the cleaning and cooking. Sometimes, in the evenings, she sits with the children while their parents go to town meetings or visiting.

Mary Elizabeth asked, "Which family do you live with?"

"Oh, I don't live with anyone. I live by myself in my own house."

"They give you your own house?"

Carrie could tell from Mary Elizabeth's appearance that she had just arrived in town. For her to not understand about my house suggests that she is a stranger, Carrie thought. Carrie instantly liked Mary Elizabeth. Her impression was that Mary Elizabeth looked like a nice young woman. Although her clothes looked ragged and faded, she was clean. Carrie noticed that Mary Elizabeth didn't have a bag or personal belongings other than the boots and the coat she was carrying over her arm. Carrie guessed that Mary Elizabeth just wandered into town with no place to stay. She looks hungry and is way too thin. Carrie decided to invite Mary Elizabeth to her house for the night. She would give her a meal and a place to sleep and see what tomorrow brings with this young stranger. If tomorrow brings on any suspicions, Carry would simply tell Mary Elizabeth that she would have to move on. In addition, Carrie lived alone and looked forward to the company.

"Why don't you come home with me for a meal and a night's sleep? I'll explain my work to you," Carrie said.

Without even thinking, Mary Elizabeth quickly and gratefully accepted the offer. For the first time in more than a year, she had a warm, home-cooked meal, a drinking glass, eating utensils and a real plate. For the first time in her life, she

35

actually spent the night sleeping in a real bed. Before going to sleep, she prayed. She thanked God for sending the angels, she thanked Him for a perfect day and for Carrie, too. Then she asked God to look after the soldiers and to forgive her for stealing the coat and boots. She wondered if the soldiers missed her.

CHAPTER 7

Carrie's house is nice. It sits on a tree-lined alley about a half-block off the main street in a row of four or five houses on each side of the alley. All the houses are just like Carrie's. "Only colored people live in the alley," Carrie said. "We all have jobs and go to work every day." Carrie is the only person who lives alone in the alley. All the other houses have families with children. Carrie's house has a parlor, a dining room and kitchen on the first floor. The second floor has a wide hallway leading to three large bedrooms. The house is furnished nicely and kept neat and clean. Nothing appeared expensive but everything appeared comfortable. Mary Elizabeth was impressed that a Negro woman had her own house, and such a nice house at that! This was more than Mary Elizabeth ever imagined and she hoped that Carrie liked her and will let her stay.

Carrie told Mary Elizabeth that there were about twenty colored families in town. They lived in their own neighborhood, separate from the whites, and all lived within a block or two from her. They have their own school and church. They were free to walk the streets and shop anywhere they wanted as long as they paid with cash. But the colored could not eat in local restaurants or use the public restrooms that were set up around the town square. If the women worked, they had jobs like Carrie, but most of them stayed home with the children. The men worked as gardeners for the rich whites, some worked in factories and some worked for the town. Colored men who worked for the town cleaned up trash and shoveled horse droppings. They maintained the streets and kept the bushes and trees around the four corners trimmed and the sidewalks swept. In the winter they shoveled snow. Carrie told Mary Elizabeth that she wished more colored women worked away from home because she has more jobs than she can handle. Carrie secretly thought to herself that she hoped Mary Elizabeth will stay around. Maybe she will share the demand for housekeepers. Carrie would keep this thought to herself for a few days, and if Mary Elizabeth turned out to be clean and honest, maybe Carrie will offer her a home and help her find work. That is, if she pays her share of the living expenses. The lord knows, Carrie could use the help.

Mary Elizabeth never heard about Negros being called colored people. She made a mental note to remember to ask Carrie about the confusion. Mary Elizabeth wondered if Carrie ever heard the "N" word, the name the bosses use for slaves back in Atlanta. And sometimes, when one slave is angry at another, they would use that awful word too. Mary Elizabeth's mouth simply couldn't say that word. "Colored isn't so bad," she thought. "Whites are white and, after all, we Negros do have color to our skin."

Within the first few days that Mary Elizabeth was in town, the Rebel troops that she had spent the past year and a half with marched right through the four corners. With their rifles in hand, they shot at random, mostly in the air or at buildings. She could see William leading the march and wondered if he had seen her. If he did, he paid her no mind. He kept on marching, looking like a mean and hateful soldier. He looked like he didn't have a compassionate bone in his body, but Mary Elizabeth knew better. All the troops bore the look of hate on their faces. She had often seen them in battle, but never before had she seen this nasty side of them. She knew they were only kids and probably are as scared as the townspeople. They just want to make noise and torment, she thought. She knew they normally marched around small towns; they always had orders to never, ever, intentionally scare or fire at civilians, especially women and children. Mary Elizabeth had no idea why they came this way, but she did know that they weren't here with the intention to shoot anyone. They probably had orders to be someplace north of here and decided to have a little fun on the way. They probably planned on displaying those unnatural nasty, mean-looking faces just to see if they would be effective and to let people know who was in charge. Mary Elizabeth felt a lump in her throat; she figured it was because seeing the soldiers again made her feel guilty. "Did I abandon them?" she said quietly to herself. They protected her over the past year and a half, and she missed them. She was grateful for what they had done for her and wondered where they will sleep tonight, what they will eat. Mary Elizabeth felt sorry; after all, they are just young kids being forced to act like mean grown men. They freeze and starve and never know from one day to the next if they will die. She wondered if they knew what they were fighting for. She never figured it out.

The display only lasted a few minutes, and the only damage noticed after the troops were gone was the six or eight bullet holes left in the pillars on the porch of the large red brick building that Mary Elizabeth still couldn't identify. The "invasion," as it was called, was the talk of the town for months. The stories grew bigger and better each time it was passed along from one person to the next. The people were sure that the troops would return, burn the town and kill everybody in sight. The men took turns watching the outer boundaries of town and even organized a night watch. Mary Elizabeth wanted to tell them that the soldiers never fought at night, but she knew better than to say anything. "Besides, who would listen to a stupid young Negro anyway?" she asked herself. Mary Elizabeth had no bad feelings concerning the "storming of the troops." She found it exciting and forgiving. Eventually the folks will settle down and the streets will be alive with shoppers and business will go on as usual, she thought to herself.

CHAPTER 8

As the days and weeks passed, Carrie and Mary Elizabeth never spoke about how long Mary Elizabeth would stay at Carrie's house. Each day went onto the next, and soon Mary Elizabeth was going to work with Carrie. Mary Elizabeth quickly learned how hard heavy housekeeping work really is. Scrubbing floors, moving heavy furniture and washing walls was the hardest work she has ever done. Not to mention reaching those high windows and gingerly cleaning all those little flowers and grooves in the silver. She hated shining silver. She remembered how her back hurt when she worked in the cotton fields, but nothing compared to this. She was glad she didn't have to look forward to working in the main house in Atlanta any longer. The families didn't mind Mary Elizabeth coming in with Carrie; they were getting two hard workers for the price of one, and besides, they liked her. They referred her to their friends and neighbors, and soon Mary Elizabeth had work of her own. Carrie was pleased with Mary Elizabeth's progress, and it was taken for granted that the two women would go on living together.

Mary Elizabeth was ecstatic to be earning her own money. She didn't know where to keep it. She knew it was valuable and didn't want to lose it, so she hid her money under her mattress. Keeping her money to herself created a dilemma for Carrie. Mary Elizabeth never saw money before, let alone have her own. She didn't know what to do with it or how to spend it.

Because Carrie liked Mary Elizabeth so much, she was patient and decided to, on occasion, just have casual conversation about money. Since Carrie was known to gossip, she would think nothing of making up stories about people and their money. One day she would talk to Mary Elizabeth about what she thought other people did with their money. Another day she would talk about the importance of money and why people work so hard to earn it. Sometimes, she went into detail explaining how some people don't have enough money to pay for food or the house they live in or the money they need to pay their taxes. Mary Elizabeth never heard about taxes. She never heard of someone selling taxes. She did, however, think when she went to market with Carrie that money exchanged hands. When Carrie put food into her basket, she gave the farmer money. Sometimes, the farmer gave her some back. "Now what kind of sense does that make?" she thought out loud to herself. Mary Elizabeth finally realized she should give Carrie some of her money. "After all, I do see Carrie giving her hard-earned money for the food that I eat." With the money situation solved, the two got along perfectly and became very close, almost like sisters. They worked hard during the day, had supper together and spent their evenings gossiping.

Carrie told Mary Elizabeth that she lived in this house with her parents. Her father passed when she was very young and so she worked along with her mother to help meet expenses. Carrie's mother passed on when Carrie was only eighteen, and since then she has been living alone and has worked long, hard hours so she could keep the house. Mary Elizabeth never saw Carrie give anyone money for the house. She wondered how that worked. Mary Elizabeth told Carrie about the plantation, the battle in Atlanta and the trip north with the soldiers. She told Carrie about the hunger, the cold and the battles. She confessed that she knew the troops who marched through town shooting at everything but the people. Carrie wasn't surprised. "Pennsylvania has more slaves traveling through on the black market than any other northern state." She told Mary Elizabeth the local restaurant owners put food out at night, expecting that some poor hungry slave would be wandering through looking for something to eat. Usually the food was gone by morning.

Even though Mary Elizabeth never asked, she thought that Carrie was probably in her late fifties or maybe early sixties. She was graying around the temples, wore her hair in a bun and kept it under control with hair pins. Her hands were rough and strong, confirming Carrie's story that she had worked hard all her life. She was short and chunky in comparison to Mary Elizabeth and most of her teeth were gone. Her skin was dry and wrinkled, and Mary Elizabeth lovingly thought that she looked like an old, dried-up potato. Lately Carrie has been very tired when she comes from a day's work. She told Mary Elizabeth that she had to rest her old bones and needed to sit in her rocker for a few minutes. Mary Elizabeth didn't mind. Cooking supper while chatting over the day with Carrie was quite relaxing. She was eager to help at home and was prepared to work harder at her jobs. Someday, when Carrie was too old to work, she knew she would have to earn enough money to take care of Carrie and the house in the same well-kept manner as Carrie had always done.

During one of their evening conversations, they were talking about town growth and about some of the influential people who lived there. Carrie told Mary Elizabeth, "The biggest thing to ever happen in this town, besides the few minutes the Rebel troops came through, is what the town counsel calls 'a day of democracy.' When the morning market first started, just a few farmers brought their horses and wagons into town every Saturday morning. They worked hard to set up their tables and put their fresh fruits and homegrown vegetables on display. They hoped to sell all they had brought and most times they did. People would swarm like flies into the four corners to shop. It became so successful that soon farmers came from all around. It was quite a sight. But town counsel didn't approve of the horses being so close to the churches and town hall. They claimed the horse droppings caused extra work for the town employees, causing higher wages. They roped the area off so the farmers couldn't park their wagons or have a place to set up their produce. As a result, the farmers had to stop coming. The townspeople went into such a fury that counsel had no choice but to reconsider. Members of town counsel called the people's display of disagreement peaceful demonstration.

"When the counsel chairman gave his speech on the steps of town hall to inform the people of his decision to allow the market to continue, he told the citizens that, 'his people are free. We live in a free northern country, not like the people of the south.' He said that, 'if this disagreement had happened in the south, southern citizens would have had to fight and some would have died because southern counsels are not willing to give their people what they ask for. This is why the north is in battle with the south, southern people need to be freed,' he said." Carrie told Mary Elizabeth that the town was the county seat and sometimes there are big murder trials at the courthouse. Mary Elizabeth soon learned that the big red brick building she couldn't identify when she first arrived was the courthouse. "When there is a big trial, the townspeople gather around the courthouse to wait and see if the criminal is guilty. They come with their children, blankets and picnic baskets. They visit around the courthouse just like they do on Sunday after church."

Carrie said that many of the houses where she cleans are owned by lawyers who have offices in the courthouse, and the lawyers' wives are always among the crowd who come with picnic baskets. "The women wanted to see if their husband won or lost a case. That way, the women will know what kind of mood they could expect from their man when he came home from work that evening." While Carrie was chuckling at her own statement, Mary Elizabeth's mind was concentrating on the possibility of finding more work. Even though she had never been inside an office, she had seen pictures of the businessmen, all dressed up in suits and bow ties, displayed on tables and mantels when she cleaned their houses. Mary Elizabeth wondered if anyone cleaned those fancy offices and who washed those huge windows. She knew the family cook always had lunch ready for the men when they came home to eat at noon, and so she determined with a grin there would be no silver to shine. She decided to visit the courthouse, and if she was bold enough, she would ask the lawyers if they were interested in having her clean their offices.

CHAPTER 9

On Tuesdays, Mary Elizabeth cleaned the office of Thomas S. Whitcomb, Esquire. Attorney Whitcomb was impressed when Mary Elizabeth knocked on his door to inquire about work. He knew it took a lot of courage for her. He was equally impressed with the way she was prepared to talk about her experience and answer questions about herself. He could find no reason to turn her down.

Attorney Whitcomb appeared to be in his late forties, graying at the temples, and wore wire rim glasses. She admired his distinguished appearance and his soft-spoken manner. He had shelf after shelf of what he called law books. There was a large wooden desk with a huge matching chair that swivelled from side to side when he moved. She noticed a few pictures on the walls but no pictures of family. His desk was cluttered, papers and books everywhere, but she thought that was probably the way it was supposed to look. He spent most of his time reading his law books and writing on a large notepad. Mary Elizabeth thought that he must be very successful. He was always friendly and always talked to Mary Elizabeth while she worked. On occasion he would offer her coffee. She gracefully declined.

One Tuesday he said, "Mary Elizabeth, will you plan to spend more time here on your next scheduled cleaning day? I would like more attention given to the floors and my desk is such a mess."

"Yes sir, I will plan longer for next Tuesday," she answered.

For the next few weeks Mary Elizabeth scraped wax and re-waxed the floor, shined and re-shined the huge wooden desk until it glistened. The windows sparkled, and there was no silver to clean. He was pleased. Spending the extra time in Attorney Whitcomb's office put her behind schedule on Tuesdays, and she often got home long after Carrie had gone to bed. Mary Elizabeth worried about Carrie every Tuesday. She worried that Carrie might be too tired to fix her own supper, she worried that Carrie might be too tired to go up the stairs, or maybe she had fallen while trying the stairs alone. In the long run Mary Elizabeth knew that her long hours would prove to be best for Carrie. In the meantime, she would have to stop worrying so much.

Mary Elizabeth knew the attorney watched her while she cleaned, and she liked that kind of attention. She began to feel a special fondness for Attorney Whitcomb and could not wait for Tuesdays. One day he said, "Mary Elizabeth, your work is superb. Would you mind if I thanked you with a hug?"

"Oh no, Mr. Whitcomb! I couldn't do that, it wouldn't be proper."

"But I like your work and I like you. I see nothing wrong with a thankful hug."

Mary Elizabeth agreed, and so they hugged. She liked it; she liked Tuesdays.

CHAPTER 10

The weekly routine of hugging was soon followed by kissing and fondling. Mary Elizabeth knew this wasn't the right thing to be doing, but she savored the attention. She began to participate and encourage the caressing and touching. She wanted to contribute to Attorney Whitcomb's enjoyment and wanted to convey her desire for him. He was becoming more aggressive with the touching, and she didn't discourage him. Sometimes, he removed her dress and kissed her neck and breasts. She became very excited and knew she would allow whatever might happen between them. Soon she was experiencing the most satisfying sex she had ever encountered. It was much more accommodating than in the tents with the soldiers. Attorney Whitcomb was even more kind and gentle than William.

She shuddered at the thought that someone might find out and worried about the consequences. This had to remain her secret; she couldn't even tell Carrie. She was comfortable with the arrangement and didn't want it to end. Besides, the attorney was considerate and loving and paid her three times as much for the pleasure than she had earned cleaning. No matter what happened, she would continue with her Tuesday schedule.

Mary Elizabeth was always anxious to make money. Word got around the courthouse that there was someone willing to clean offices. She was hired by two additional lawyers. Of course, she began by cleaning, but when the lawyers noticed the added personal attention she gave, such as brushing lint from their suit coats, or the way her body moved when serving coffee or waxing the desk, they couldn't help but return the attention.

Mary Elizabeth envisioned earning enough money so Carrie could limit her work to sitting with children and not have to continue with the heavy work much longer. If Mary Elizabeth continued to play her cards right, maybe she could entice other attorneys or maybe even doctors. She will be more careful about how she dressed, find different ways to fix her hair, and become more conversational. She will add a few alluring movements that she is sure will attract attention. She knows she is considered attractive, and with minor improvements, she could make herself so intriguing that she would not go unnoticed.

Within the next few months, Mary Elizabeth's tactics worked, and her business grew. She was no longer a cleaning person but a very well-paid prostitute. Her "clients" were respectable citizens with large sums of money, and they appreciated her attention. Now that things are going so well for her, she wanted to take on more obligation at home. She proposed to Carrie that she slow down and spend more time baby-sitting. Carrie didn't comment. She continued to maintained her busy schedule as usual. This concerned Mary Elizabeth. Maybe her secret was more conspicuous than she realized, but the subject was never discussed between the two.

By the age of twenty, Mary Elizabeth was a very successful business woman. She had more money then she ever dreamed possible. She was able to choose her clientele and limit herself to just three jobs per day. She could have more work if she wanted but preferred to take time between clients to go home, bathe, and spend time primping before going to the next job. Cleanliness was most important to her, and she expected the same of her clients. She catered to doctors, lawyers, college professors and even the chief of police. She didn't spend much of her money and continued to hide it around the house. After two years, and with Carrie's encouragement, Mary Elizabeth finally learned that a certain amount of shopping was necessary. Carrie taught her the importance of keeping herself presentable, and that meant buying a new dress from time to time. Carrie couldn't, however, convince Mary Elizabeth that she should buy a pair of shoes. Mary Elizabeth bought just enough to keep herself presentable.

Now that Mary Elizabeth has a new profession, she is more concerned about how she looks. She purchased a few new dresses, nothing fancy. She wanted to be sure she always had a fresh dress when the others needed laundered. She also bought a few toiletries, items like a light-colored lipstick and perfume. The most uncomfortable item she purchased, and with Carrie's blessing, was one pair of new shoes that hurt her feet. She laughed at the thought that her work didn't require that she keep shoes on her sore feet. Carrie often commented to Mary Elizabeth about how nice she looked. Mary Elizabeth worried about the compliment. She was concerned that Carrie might be suspicious.

CHAPTER 11

Mary Elizabeth had been working steadily for almost a year now, but for the past few weeks she hadn't been feeling well. She was sick in her stomach and had very little energy. Carrie insisted that Mary Elizabeth visit her doctor. They were sure she had the flu and Carrie's doctor said as much. Still, in the weeks that followed, Mary Elizabeth's illness didn't improve. Mary Elizabeth knew that she has missed her monthly, and she remembered the women in the fields back in Atlanta talking about what happens when a women misses her monthly. There's a baby on the way, they always said. A return trip to Carrie's doctor confirmed her suspicion that she was pregnant. "How could this have happened?" she asked herself. As William had taught her, she had always been careful. She couldn't remember ever, not once, having a client not willing to withdraw. Her pregnancy was another secret she had to keep from Carrie for as long as possible.

Mary Elizabeth will have to begin planning. She will have to take a few months away from work, and at the same time figure out a way to save her business. She must continue to earn an income; she owes it to Carrie. The only way she could possibly make it work is to find someone interested in working for her. "I wonder if that kind of person even exists?" she asked herself. She decided she would let it be known around town that she was looking for a young female to help look after Carrie. Carrie was aging quickly, and against her wishes she was forced to cut her work to three days per week. Finding someone to help with Carrie and do light housework and light cooking would appear logical.

"I'm Martha Neidigh; I hear you're looking for someone to help with housekeeping." Mary Elizabeth was polite and talked to her, but knew instantly that Martha was not the kind of person she was looking for. Martha said she was eighteen and had experience cooking and washing dishes at a local restaurant. Mary Elizabeth listened but knew she was more interested in appearance and personality then past work experience. Martha was grossly overweight and in serious need of improving her grooming. She was missing a front tooth and kinda spit when she spoke. Mary Elizabeth told Martha that she wasn't ready to hire anybody just yet, but would let her know in a few weeks. There had been more of the same from people on the streets asking about the job. Some were old and could barely get around, some were only children, twelve or thirteen. What struck Mary Elizabeth as very strange was that none of the inquiries came from colored. "Isn't this funny," she said proudly to herself, "white people asking a colored woman for work?" Mary Elizabeth remembered Carrie saying that the colored women in town didn't want to work. How true Carrie's statement proved to be, she thought to herself. When looking for the right person, Mary Elizabeth had certain qualifications in mind. She thought that age was more important than color, but hygiene and appearance was most important. She needed someone who could carry on a decent conversation and someone who was interested in working hard. Mary Elizabeth knew exactly what she was looking for and felt comfortable knowing she has several months before she needed to make a decision. She would take her time and choose just the right person.

Like any other Saturday, Mary Elizabeth attended market.

If Carrie wasn't feeling up to it, Mary Elizabeth shopped alone. She felt proud carrying her own basket and shopping for fresh fruits and vegetables with her own money. The heavier her basket, the happier she was. She always bought fresh flowers to take home to Carrie. Carrie would say: "Good lord child, how do you think we can ever use all this stuff? And why the flowers, do you think money grows on trees?" On the days that Carrie felt good, she and Mary Elizabeth attended market together. They always spent the entire morning tasting the goodies, smelling the fresh flowers and visiting with Carrie's friends. They always had someone to gossip about when they returned home, and while putting their purchases away, they chattered and giggled like two little school girls. Carrie always had stories about the people they had just seen; some were sad stories, but most made Mary Elizabeth laugh. When Carrie was able, spending those Saturday mornings together was the highlight of Mary Elizabeth's week.

On this particular Saturday, Carrie wasn't feeling well. Mary Elizabeth was a little sad about Carrie's health; she tried to concentrate on her shopping but she couldn't stop thinking about Carrie and her illness. She knew she was missing another interesting story about a particular person or a long legend on how town used to be. She especially missed the laughing and hoped she could overhear some gossip to share with Carrie when she got home. Suddenly, her spirits were lifted when she spotted a very attractive young woman at a nearby bakery table. The woman didn't appear to be shopping; probably she was just taking in the sights, the same as Mary Elizabeth had done the first day she arrived in town. This looks exactly like the kind of person she wanted to work for her. Her appearance was striking. She appeared to be in her late teens or early twenties. Beautiful long, curly blond hair. She was tall and thin and was as fresh to look at as the flowers Mary Elizabeth was about to buy. Since this is a college town, Mary Elizabeth assumed that the pretty blond might be a college student. "How does a colored woman who appears to be a servant approach this confident-looking and attractive young woman?" Mary Elizabeth quietly said to herself. Then she remembered two and a half years ago when Carrie approached her and said good morning. Mary Elizabeth walked over to the bakery table and said:

"Good morning, are you enjoying the market?"

"Yes I am. I've never seen anything like this."

"Well, I'm glad. My name is Mary Elizabeth Thompson. (She had never used a last name before and she knew Carrie wouldn't mind). It's nice to meet you. Are you visiting?"

"No, I'm just starting my first year at the law school. I will be here for three years."

Mary Elizabeth responded: "I hope you enjoy your time here, and the college too."

There was a pause, and Mary Elizabeth was concerned about how to keep the conversation going. She wasn't sure what to say next.

The girl finally said, "I'm Katherine Brownington. I'm from Baltimore. I'm sure I will like it here better when I find something to keep me busy."

Mary Elizabeth jumped at the opportunity. "There is lots of work here. Are you looking for a job?"

"I will need to work while I'm in school, but I haven't started looking yet."

"Maybe some of the doctors and lawyers I clean for have work for you. I can introduce you to them if you want."

They arranged to meet the following Tuesday at Attorney Whitcomb's office.

The meeting went as Mary Elizabeth planned. She

introduced Katherine to the lawyer, telling him that Katherine was looking for work while attending law school. She asked if he could give her a desk job. Attorney Whitcomb studied Katherine very closely. He liked what he saw and thought that a law student would be a real asset to his office. Mary Elizabeth could tell he was interested. To no surprise, he agreed to hire her. She will work on Fridays. Mary Elizabeth was sure that any additional requirements on the job would come about naturally. They dismissed Katherine and, with pleasure, Mary Elizabeth performed her usual Tuesday morning commitment.

Even though Mary Elizabeth still visited Attorney Whitcomb on Tuesdays, she didn't want to ask about Katherine. She knew she would find out in due time on her own. After a few weeks had passed, Mary Elizabeth ran into Katherine at market. Katherine reported that she was only working a few hours on Fridays and was pleased with her duties. Mary Elizabeth wasted no time offering her more of the same. "However, Katherine, you must agree to allow me to arrange your interviews and act as your employer." Katherine quickly agreed; nothing more needed to be said. They each knew what the other was doing.

Mary Elizabeth's pregnancy is beginning to show. She was forced to stop working and stay at home with Carrie. With the money she had saved, and having Katherine working for her, the household was supported nicely. After the baby came, Mary Elizabeth would return to work, keep Katherine employed if she wanted to stay, and hire a full-time housekeeper to stay with Carrie and the baby.

CHAPTER 12

Cory Elizabeth Thompson was born March 12, 1867. Childbirth was not easy for Mary Elizabeth. Her muscles were shaky and she lost a lot of blood. She needed time to rest and stayed in bed for three days. "I wonder how those women in Atlanta, who gave birth in the fields, could go on working," she said to Carrie. She told Carrie that giving birth in the fields was so common that new mothers said they felt like cows. "Just drop it in the field and leave it. The boss will be coming to take it away." Female slaves knew that after giving birth, the baby would be taken to the big house and nursed by a nanny. They never saw their baby again. After the age of five, the children would become workers. Of course, by then, mothers would not know which child might be hers.

"She is the most gorgeous baby I ever laid my eyes on," Carrie said enthusiastically. During the pregnancy, Carrie never asked questions. Even though Mary Elizabeth had not worked for several months, the money kept coming in. Even though it was obvious to Carrie that a baby was on the way, she would not ask. "It is so strange," Carrie said to herself, "we always talked about everything. Maybe some things don't need to be said." Carrie sat for hours rocking and singing to little Cory while Mary Elizabeth busied herself with the household chores. Mary Elizabeth knew that when she returned to work, a baby-sitter would not be an immediate concern, but she would need a housekeeper and probably should start looking soon.

As Cory grew stronger, Carrie grew weaker. One morning when Cory was just four weeks old, Carrie simply did not wake up from her sleep. The doctor said it was from old age and natural causes. He said it was a comfortable passing for Carrie. "She probably didn't suffer from pain. When she took her last breath she was in a relaxed sleeping state." He said: "I've noticed that in the past few months since I've been seeing Carrie regularly, she seemed very content. I don't remember a time in all the years I've been her doctor that I have ever seen her so satisfied and so at ease with herself." The doctor went on to tell Mary Elizabeth that she and little Cory changed Carrie's long, lonely life to a new life of joy and happiness. "She passed on a happy women," he said.

The next few weeks were chaotic for Mary Elizabeth. Not only was she feeling depressed about Carrie's death, she still hadn't fully recovered from childbirth. A constant flow of Carrie's friends and employers arrived day after day to pay their respects. Mary Elizabeth was completely exhausted. The visitors brought food and flowers, some even brought money. Additional pressure resulted because Mary Elizabeth worked for the husbands, and Carrie worked for the wives and children of those who were visiting. It was uncomfortable for her to see her employers together with their families. Mary Elizabeth wondered if any of the children here could be a brother or sister to Cory. She watched the men look at Cory as if each was convinced that the baby was his. Of course, Mary Elizabeth is not sure who the father is either and found herself comparing the men to Cory. Cory was very light-skinned and her hair was dark brown. She had the features of a white baby, but of course a darker complexion. She is small like her mother and has her mother's high cheekbones. But unlike her mother, her eyes are shaped like almonds, her lips are slim and her jaw is square.

She is a good baby and absolutely beautiful. Anyone who looked at Cory knew she had not been fathered by a Negro. Mary Elizabeth wondered what her mother looked like and if she had felt the same uneasiness when she gave birth to her. Did her mother know who had fathered her child?

Now that Carrie is gone, Mary Elizabeth is on her own. Katherine continues to provide income, not as much as Mary Elizabeth had been accustomed to, but Mary Elizabeth still has money hidden and can fare comfortably for another month or so. She will stay home with Cory until she is able to find a suitable baby-sitter.

Only a few days after Carrie's funeral, Attorney Whitcomb came to visit. He explained that he felt a responsibility and was concerned for the welfare of her and the baby. He never did say he thought Cory was his daughter, but Mary Elizabeth could tell by his sincerity that he was certain. Secretly, Mary Elizabeth hoped he was right. Others came for the same reason; they would ooh and aah over Cory and sometimes even ask to hold her. They offered money to pay a baby-sitter if Mary Elizabeth wanted to return to work. They brought gifts for Mary Elizabeth, clothing and toys for Cory. Mary Elizabeth would not accept money, but she loved the gifts and had so much fun dressing Cory in the beautiful, tiny ruffled dresses. Cory had more fancy dresses than Mary Elizabeth will ever have in her whole lifetime. There was so much affection shown toward Cory by these men that Mary Elizabeth sometimes become overwhelmed with emotion. She was known to shed a tear or two, or initiate a hug to convey her gratitude. She decided that someday she will tell Cory that her father was a kind and gentle man. The visits continued, the display of gratitude intensified and soon Mary Elizabeth was back in business.

CHAPTER 13

The town was growing rapidly. In the past year a new hospital was built and the courthouse was expanded to a second floor. The county commissioners were even considering building a second courthouse on the empty lot at the four corners. The law school doubled in size, and with it came more students and more professors. As the community grew, so did Mary Elizabeth's business. She employed two additional students, and Katherine is still working for her. Katherine will graduate in the spring but has not decided if she will stay, or eventually start her own business at home in Baltimore. Since Carrie's death, and with legal help from Attorney Whitcomb, Mary Elizabeth has taken over the taxes on the house and had the deed changed into her name. The business is now carried on from Mary Elizabeth's house. The girls have their own rooms and each their own clientele. The girls keep twenty-five percent of the money earned and Mary Elizabeth gets the remaining seventy-five. Mary Elizabeth is making so much money that she's not sure what to do with it all. She doesn't want to use the bank. She thought that would create suspicion, so she continues to hide her money in the house. She plans to keep her business small and secret from the townspeople. When Mary Elizabeth goes out to shop, she dresses Cory in her expensive matching outfits and pushes her around town in an exceptionally beautiful baby carriage (a gift from Attorney Whitcomb). It appears to the public that Mary Elizabeth is the nanny for a very well-to-do family. The assumptions please Mary Elizabeth. What people assume helps her to keep her business subtle. Keeping it quiet and unnoticed is for Cory's benefit.

CHAPTER 14

Now that Cory is fifteen, Mary Elizabeth allows her to answer the door and receive customers. If the man has to wait, Cory offers him coffee or something cold to drink. She sits in the front parlor chatting with him and is a natural at making him feel comfortable. She also collects the money. Cory isn't disturbed about her mother's business; it's the only thing she has ever known and accepts it as a normal way of life. Mary Elizabeth is, however, very watchful of Cory. Cory is very beautiful. Her brown skin is smooth and clear, her eyes are big and bright, and her long, curly hair reflects a healthy shine. She is tall and slim and displays the appearance of a healthy, bright and confident young woman. She is quite advanced for her age; most people think she is older than fifteen. Clients often asked if Cory is available. Cory and her mother are satisfied with Cory's current role and have no plans to expand her responsibilities at such a young age. Mary Elizabeth hopes that someday Cory will take over the business.

CHAPTER 15

The older Cory gets, the more beautiful she becomes. She has lots of friends but they are never invited to the house. She is now in high school and has outgrown her interest in the business. She spends most of her time away from home with her friends. Mary Elizabeth wonders if Cory is embarrassed by her mother's establishment. After finishing high school, Cory is never home during the day. She leaves in the morning and returns in the evening just in time to go to bed. She very seldom spends time with Mary Elizabeth. When they do have a few minutes to talk, the only subject Cory is interested in talking about is her new boyfriend. Mary Elizabeth realizes that her daughter is growing up and soon she will be an adult. She probably is old enough for love, Mary Elizabeth thinks to herself. Like all mothers, Mary Elizabeth must concede to the realization that the space in her daughter's heart, the same space usually reserved for mothers, must now be shared with someone else. That someone else is Cory's boyfriend, Joel Jackson. Joel finished high school two years before Cory and is considered to be from one of the better colored families in town.

When Joel isn't working, he spends every free minute he has with Cory. It would be unusual to see one without the other. They are the talk of the town. They are both so attractive that they turn heads when they walk the streets. People call them "the perfect couple." When Cory turned nineteen, she and Joel were married. Joel has a good job with the local railroad switch company. His pay is above average for a colored man and so he was able to purchase a house in preparation for the upcoming wedding. He wanted things to be just perfect for the day he brought his new wife home. Cory had begun to move her things into Joel's house weeks before the wedding. She wanted to be prepared so that when she became Mrs. Joel Jackson, she would have nothing else to think about except devoting herself to being Joel's wife. Mary Elizabeth wanted to give Cory and Joel a church wedding and reserve a local restaurant to serve a meal to the invited guests. But she and Cory decided it would be best not to flaunt. Only rich people, and never the colored, have church weddings. Mary Elizabeth always dreamt of giving Cory a beautiful wedding but could not take the chance of openly displaying her success. The wedding took place in Joel's backyard. After the ceremony and when the guests began to leave, Mary Elizabeth felt sad to think that Cory would not be going home with her. Cory is already home. Mary Elizabeth felt the emptiness.

Even though Cory and Joel live just two blocks away, Cory visits her mother only one or two days a week. Joel never visits; in fact, Joel has never been inside his mother-in-law's house. Mary Elizabeth understands and realizes that her surroundings probably would not be comfortable for Joel. Mary Elizabeth can see the happiness in Cory's eyes and is glad for her, but she misses Cory terribly and wishes they could spend more time together. Many times the visits are interrupted by clients, and Cory resents the interruptions. She doesn't look forward to visiting her mother.

Now that Cory is married, she feels sorry for her mother. She is very happy. Life is so perfect for her that she feels a little guilty. Cory realizes that she possesses a kind of happiness that her mother most likely never had the chance to experience.

She adores Joel and cherishes every minute she spends with him. He is gentle, loving and very kind. He is tall and handsome and incredibly smart. Joel has a good job, works hard and is always cheerful and happy. Her friends tell her they are jealous. They say, "He was considered the catch of town." They all admitted to having a crush on him at one time or another and often wished Joel would have given them a chance. Now that he's married and beams with happiness, they are glad for him and Cory. Cory wonders if her mother ever felt this much love for anyone. She sometimes wonders about her father and asks herself why she never had the chance to meet him. Cory has never built up the courage to ask her mother.

Joel likes to tell funny stories just to watch Cory laugh. She laughs so hard that her sides hurt and tears roll down her cheeks. Joel hugs her, picks her up and spins her around until they are both laughing together. These are precious moments to Cory, moments she will never forget. Cory remembers being happy as a child but doesn't remember if she ever really laughed. She has decided that life couldn't be any better then this. They are a genuine example of "the perfect couple," as the townspeople continue to call them. When Cory discovered she was pregnant, she was ecstatic. Joel was so excited that everyone he saw, even if it was a stranger on the street, he would proudly announce, while touching Cory's belly, "I'm going to be a daddy." Cory would laugh.

Mary Elizabeth was happy for them, but she knew now that any chance of Cory taking over the business has now vanished. Cory is content being a wife, and with the news that she is to become a mother, she is more radiant than ever. Cory never complained about feeling sick or tired. Her pregnancy, just like her life, was perfect. After a very easy nine months and exactly when expected, Cory gave birth to a beautiful healthy daughter,

Rebecca Mary Jackson.

Cory continued to visit Mary Elizabeth, but the visits were fewer and less time spent with each stay. Cory explained to Mary Elizabeth that she is not comfortable exposing her daughter to her mother's environment, and this is the reason for fewer visits. Mary Elizabeth's feelings were hurt. She tried to understand, but the emptiness she felt would not go away. Two years later, when Cory gave birth to her second daughter, Marian Elizabeth Jackson, all visits stopped. Mary Elizabeth's heart was very heavy. She adored her granddaughters, but realized she couldn't interfere with Cory's commitment to protect her children from their grandmother's business. If she wanted to see her grandchildren, she would have to be the one to take the initiative. So every Sunday, she visited with Joel, Cory and her two beautiful granddaughters. Joel knew of his mother-in-law's profession, and like Cory, didn't approve, but he was happy to welcome Mary Elizabeth into his home. He thought that no matter how Cory was conceived, he loved her and thanked his mother-in-law, and God, every day for giving him his beautiful family. The girls are cheerful and bright and almost as lovely as their mother, Mary Elizabeth thought to herself. She relished her visits. She has never seen such a happy family.

Rebecca is almost ten now and Marian eight. Soon they will be old enough to visit their grandmother on their own if they want. This has always been a secret wish for Mary Elizabeth. She fantasized about having her granddaughters to herself and away from the protection of their mother. Sometimes she visualized the girls sitting at her kitchen table, sharing cookies, talking about anything they felt like talking about and laughing. Within her mind, Mary Elizabeth could hear the laugher; she doesn't remember hearing anyone laugh in this house since

Carrie. She would have to be careful, though; she couldn't allow the customers to see her granddaughters. Admitting to her clients that she was old enough to be a grandmother was an extremely difficult task for Mary Elizabeth to think about. She was proud of her appearance and looked much younger than her fifty- two years. If she allowed her age to show, she would lose business. And yet she knew if she wanted to be a real grandmother, she would have to make some changes in her lifestyle. After pondering the situation over for a few days, her solution was to bring in more working girls. Mary Elizabeth will no longer "work." She will serve as Cory once did. She will greet the gentlemen, offer them drinks and converse with them if they had to wait. She will serve as "madam" of the house. However, she will still cater to Attorney Whitcomb. He has remained especially important to her over the years, not only professionally but personally too. "If my idea works, I will be free to visit with Rebecca and Marian when they come," she said to herself.

June 16th, 1901, when Rebecca was fourteen and Marian twelve, their father was killed in an accident at work. He was crushed between two railroad switches. Two men came from the switch company to give Cory the news. They politely told Cory that Joel was a good worker and they were sorry to lose him. They offered to help with the final arrangements and told Cory the wives of Joel's fellow workers would provide food for the wake, but Cory was unresponsive. Cory's friends and most of Joel's fellow employees attended the wake. Cory refused to greet them. The women came with food but Cory failed to acknowledge them. The house was crowded. Rebecca and Marian were overwhelmed; they didn't know how to greet the guest or what to say. After their father's body was removed from the house and taken for burial, Cory and the two girls returned home. The guests were gone and the house was empty without Joel. Cory sat on a chair and stared out the window. She never said a word to her daughters.

Months have passed since the wake and still Cory is unable to function. The girls have become dependent on each other and rely on their grandmother for necessities. Mary Elizabeth visits Cory as often as possible and supports the family financially, but Cory still remains unresponsive. She hasn't said a word to anyone since the day Joel died.

When the tenants who lived next door to Mary Elizabeth moved out (it was rumored that the neighbor didn't like living next door to a whore house), she ask Attorney Whitcomb to help her find out if the house was for sale, and if so, she wanted him to make arrangements for her to purchase the house. The owner was a doctor who was anxious to sell. He indicated that he would have a difficult time re-renting the house if the rumors he heard were true. The price was reasonable, and Mary Elizabeth was able to purchase with cash. Immediately after the deed transfer, and without resistance from Cory, she and the girls moved in. For the next four years, Mary Elizabeth continued to support her daughter and her two granddaughters. She hired a full-time housekeeper to stay with them and did her best to comply with Cory's wishes. She worked very hard at keeping the girls away from her establishment. When Mary Elizabeth visited with the girls, she always took them downtown shopping or to a restaurant for a treat. Rebecca, on occasion, would enter her grandmother's house unannounced through the back door and into the kitchen. Mary Elizabeth would not encourage Rebecca's visits and told her granddaughter that she was glad to see her, but, "Rebecca, you should never walk into anyone's house unannounced; it's not the polite thing to do." In 1906, as everyone expected, Cory died of a broken heart. It was hard for Mary Elizabeth to feel grief. Cory lived a lonely and sorrowful life, and she seemed to be waiting for death. Mary Elizabeth knew that Cory wanted to be with Joel. She thought that perhaps Cory's passing was a blessing.

Rebecca, now nineteen, and Marian, seventeen, handled their mother's passing well. Since Joel's death, Cory was usually found sitting alone in her room. She never spoke to her daughters; she never noticed when they came and went. She didn't even eat with them. Marian always looked in on her, but Cory ignored her daughter. They had become very separate and so the girls, understandably, didn't miss their mother.

CHAPTER 16

Rebecca was incredibly interested in what was going on at her grandmother's house, but Marian was determined to stay away. During the five years they lived next to their grandmother, they often hid in the alley and watched the men come and go. They watched girls arrive by cab and within a few days other girls leave by cab. They came and left at different times so there was always three or four girls at the house. They were intrigued with all the make-up and pretty clothes. The girls looked awfully young to be doing what Marian thought they were doing, and Rebecca found them to be extremely fascinating. Rebecca and Marian were old enough to understand the business and always heard plenty about it at school. Marian was embarrassed.

It wasn't long until Rebecca worked her way into her grandmother's door, and without really comprehending, she was involved with the business. Of course, having her around pleased Mary Elizabeth very much. Rebecca loved sitting in the parlor with the girls. She listened to the stories about the big cities they came from and about what they might do after they graduated from college. She was electrified when talking with such interesting and intelligent white college girls. "My goodness, they aren't much older then we are," she told Marian, "and yet they are so far away from home." Marian wasn't at all impressed. She didn't approve of the business. It didn't matter to Rebecca how often Marian expressed her disapproval, her interest continued to escalate. Rebecca continued to babble on and on about how she thought the girls were so brave, and how they were so far away from home. She thought they were very courageous to venture out on their own and into the kind of work they have chosen. "They make a lot of money," Rebecca told Marian. Marian became irritated with the conversation and refused to hear more. She went to her room, leaving Rebecca alone to talk to herself. Rebecca continued to spent most of her time at her grandmother's and is proud to have been "promoted." She is now allowed to greet the clients, offer them drinks and collect the money, the same as her mother had done almost twenty-two years ago. Marian stayed next door with the housekeeper.

After graduating from high school, Marian found work at the mail room in the courthouse basement. She was a loner and hardly spoke to her co-workers. She sensed that everyone knew about the family business, and she remained embarrassed by it. If she walked near a group of people who were talking, they always became quiet when they saw her coming. They seemed to continue their conversation after Marian passed. She hoped it was just coincidental, and yet, she didn't think so.

Rebecca's enthusiasm continued to grow. The goings-on in the house next door was all she talked about when she was home with Marian. She told stories about the businessmen all dressed in their coats and ties, and how sometimes there would be three or even four waiting. She told Marian about how she entertains the men while they wait and about how she has been sworn to secrecy about their identity. "Rebecca, I don't want to hear anymore. That kind of business is wrong," Marian told Rebecca. The two sisters had their first real disagreement ever. Rebecca argued that the operation is good for the family. "It will be carried over from generation to generation. Grandmother told me that," she said.

Marian told Rebecca that they were the only existing members of the next generation and that she, or her children, "will not become involved in such sinful filth." They didn't talk to each for days. Marian didn't care, she was determined not to be involved in "the family business" and she didn't want to encourage Rebecca. Marian was embarrassed to walk down the street. Her paranoia was getting the best of her. She stayed at home alone and wished that Rebecca would give up her interest in prostitution.

Marian remained quiet at work and didn't bother making friends. There was, however, one particular mail customer she liked to talk with and looked forward to seeing him each day. He was a new lawyer who had his office on the second floor of the courthouse. Marian guessed that because he was just starting his career, he probably couldn't afford to have someone work for him, and so he had to pick up his own mail. They always had something to talk about: the weather, the new construction in town or about how quickly his business is growing. Whatever the conversation, Marian was always comfortable with his presence. Lately, Attorney Ellis spent more time in the mail room than he used to.

John Ellis was rather short but very attractive. He was young, energetic, and especially polite. He didn't appear to dress as successful as the other attorneys, but he was always neat and clean. Marian thought he might be about twenty-five and probably lonely. Why else would he spend so much time in the mail room? she thought to herself. Marian looked forward to John's visits and wasn't at all concerned about what others might say. "What harm could come from open conversation between a white lawyer and a colored mail room clerk?" she quietly asked herself. One day, out of general conversation, John ask her what she did with yourself when not working. "Do you live alone? Do you have a boyfriend? Tell me about your family."

Marian was surprised at all the questions and thought he was becoming too personal, but deep down, she didn't mind answering. "I live with my sister. We used to have a housekeeper, but now that we are older, we no longer need her. So now I have the ususal cooking and housework; it keeps me busy. I do not have a boyfriend and that's just fine with me for now."

As time went on they had more personal conversations. She learned he was just out of law school, his father died recently, his mother is still living and he has no brothers or sisters. He is from Philadelphia but doesn't plan to return there because he prefers small towns. He lives alone and doesn't have a girlfriend. Marian told him about her father's death and how much in love her parents were. She told John that her mother was unable to cope with the passing of her father and, as expected, she died of a broken heart. She mentioned her grandmother and told John, "Even though I never stayed with my grandmother, she cared for me and her sister until we were old enough to be on our own." She explained, however, that her sister spends most of her time at her grandmother's, and so her evenings are quiet. He has quiet evenings also and suggested that they get together for coffee sometime.

John arrived at 6:30, just as they had agreed. Marian was nervous and again asked herself, "What harm could come from having him visit for coffee?" Deep down Marian knew she had developed special feelings for John but was not concerned about romance. Romantic thoughts never entered her mind. Besides, romance with a white man was unthinkable and forbidden. John had a different point of view: if he was infatuated with a colored woman, so be it. He was not concerned about whether his interest in Marian developed into something more permanent. He felt anxious to see her and would not be a minute late for his visit. They spent a short evening over coffee and a homemade chocolate cake that Marian had made for the occasion. They talked as usual. Marian thought how easy it is to talk with him. But having him in her house made her nervous. She hoped Rebecca didn't come home early. She hoped nobody saw him arrive. She worried about if someone would see him leave. John could tell that Marian's mind was preoccupied and that she was uneasy, so he didn't want to overstay his visit. He thanked her for the coffee and expressed his liking for the chocolate cake. He was gone within an hour. He will stay longer next time.

CHAPTER 17

Rebecca spent all her waking hours at her grandmother's. Mary Elizabeth was delighted but still felt guilty about the possibility of betraying Cory's wishes. Mary Elizabeth would never allow her granddaughter to become physically involved with the clients, and that took away some of the guilt. She was extremely pleased that Rebecca was becoming more interested each day. Mary Elizabeth noticed that Rebecca became very conscientious about who she would allow to enter. She once overheard Rebecca tell someone they couldn't enter because she thought they were too young. Rebecca told Mary Elizabeth, "You know, Grandmother, I don't think the establishment is any longer a secret around town. I think we should be more careful and screen new clients before we let them in. We should not cater to students, colored or to anyone who did not appear clean." Hygiene was an obsession with Rebecca, and sometimes she would give a waiting client a basin of water and tell him to go into the next room and clean himself. Mary Elizabeth allowed Rebecca to set the rules, and because business was often more than her girls could handle, she agreed with Rebecca that screening visitors was a good idea. They became so successful that more girls and more room was needed to meet the demand of their clients. They decided to convert the attic area into two more rooms and hire more girls. Business is thriving. Now Mary Elizabeth must find more hiding places to keep her money.

Mary Elizabeth had managed a hard life, and her energy

level was decreasing quickly. Having Rebecca around to help with decisions was a relief. Now that Rebecca has taken over the duties as madam, Mary Elizabeth has more time to herself. Sometimes she allows her mind to wander and recalls those days back in Atlanta. She often thinks of her mother. How she must have suffered when forced to give up her newborn baby. Mary Elizabeth's life changed tremendously when she gave birth to Cory; she had someone to love and someone to return that love. Did her mother ever have anyone to love? She looks back on her life and decides she will never regret what she has done. She earned her own money, saved and spent it wisely. She was financially able to care for her family when they needed her. She thought about how Carrie had given her her first break, but since then, she has made wise decisions and has earned every bit of her success on her own. She has provided nicely for her granddaughters. Rebecca will live in this house and Marian will live in the house next door. I will give each their with their own home. She is certain that leaving Atlanta was the right decision. With those thoughts she felt peace and enjoyed a good night's sleep.

Mary Elizabeth decided that the next time she sees Attorney Whitcomb, she will speak to him about her intentions. She will ask him to have the two properties changed into their prospective new owners' names. It was decided that the girls would be handed the deeds to their prospective property as a gift at Christmas time.

Marian was very appreciative when handed her gift, but Rebecca expected that someday she would have the property anyway and wasn't at all surprised. Rebecca knew that her grandmother intended for her to take over the business, and that silly piece of paper meant nothing. She did decide, however, that now with official ownership, she would set all the rules and make changes as she sees fit. Without discussing her decision with Mary Elizabeth, Rebecca simply took on all the obligations. She made all the decisions about running the business, the household, and even the distribution of Mary Elizabeth's money. Rebecca knew Mary Elizabeth hid money but never knew where and had no idea how much. But from now on, the money would be disbursed equally between Mary Elizabeth and Rebecca. Mary Elizabeth had no problem with Rebecca taking over entirely. She was glad to get rid of the responsibilities. It was her time for rest.

Mary Elizabeth is showing signs of aging. She tires quickly and has a difficult time going up and down the stairs. Going outdoors for routine shopping became impossible. Her legs hurt and she suffered from shortness of breath. Her eyesight was deteriorating quickly and she was not comfortable moving around in the house. She took to her bed and asked Rebecca to bring her meals. She also requested that Rebecca send for Attorney Whitcomb. Mary Elizabeth remembered how Carrie had become very weak and suddenly passed peacefully in her sleep. She thought that the same was about to happen to her. She wanted to meet with Attorney Whitcomb to insure that all her final preparations were in order. She instructed him on where she should be buried, what she would wear, and what her headstone would read. After all these years, she had never forgotten the angels. She requested that her headstone to be inscribed with the words: "Dancing with Angels."

After the death of Marian's grandmother, John thought he should spend more time with Marian. He sensed that Marian was not doing well and desperately missed her sister. Marian had told him that she hadn't seen Rebecca for weeks. She moved all her possessions into Mary Elizabeth's house, and the two sisters became total strangers. Although Marian never told John, having Rebecca living just next door and yet never seeing her broke Marian's heart. Still, she was determined never to set foot in that filthy, sinful house of prostitution. John knew Marian was lonely. He noticed signs of withdraw; she even missed a few days work. For Marian, that was highly unusual. He liked her a lot and wanted to spend as much time with her as he could. Marian was receptive to his visits but was usually quiet. John was worried that Marian was beginning to suffer from depression.

CHAPTER 18

Rebecca was happy to be the madam of the house. She made a few more changes, which gave her satisfaction and added to the meaning of ownership. She would serve coffee, if the client wished, and also offer alcohol. Of course, each watered down serving was at a small fee. She also supplied rubbers and insisted her girls use them. They were a quarter each. To brighten and refresh the house, Rebecca had fresh flowers delivered three times a week from the local florist. The house furniture was re-arranged and throughly cleaned. She added a bathroom upstairs and another small room downstairs with just a wash basin. She was making money. The most important change she planned was to take on more girls—only have four at a time but have them rotate. This would add variety for the customer. Katherine was still working, but Rebecca never knew when to count on her. She came and went as she pleased. Katherine worked the area for a few weeks, and when she felt like leaving, she would return to Baltimore where she worked for another madam. Rebecca wanted to phase out the college students and use full-time prostitutes who could be available any hour of the day or night. She wanted to know when the girls were coming and leaving, and so she scheduled them on two- week rotations.

Rebecca didn't tell anybody, but when she was moving her things into her grandmother's room, she opened a trunk that stood at the foot of the bed and found seventeen thousand dollars in cash. With so much money, she could do anything she wanted.

She knew that eventually she would find her grandmother's other hiding places. She wondered how much was hidden and if she would ever find it all.

CHAPTER 19

John was spending all his free time with Marian. After work they had supper together and spent their evenings in each other's company. Some nights he would go home to sleep and some nights he would sleep with Marian. Eventually he moved in and they were living together. Marian liked the idea of having John live with her; it gave her a feeling of security and yet she worried. She worried about being able to meet his expectations. Could she work and at the same time take care of the house the way she wanted to? She worried about the cleaning, the shopping and wasn't sure she could keep up. She still worried that John might be discovered entering or leaving her house. She worried about everything. One day, as though he could read her mind, John suggested to Marian that she quit her job and stay at home to take care of things around the house. And so she did. She is more relaxed now and looks forward to spending her time alone. She doesn't like to be with people. Most times, she's not very anxious for John to come home. Once in a while, when she's doing her chores, she pretends that she is playing house and that she is John's wife. Of course, she realizes they could never be married. How could they? "Colored women don't marry white men," she said to herself. "They wouldn't dare to be seen in public together, and besides, what preacher would marry them?" They must keep their arrangement a secret, so playing house and pretending to be his wife is her only alternative. Although Marian is never rude to John, she sufferers severely with mood swings. Sometimes she isn't interested in anything John says, and some days she stays in bed until noon. Her moods worry John. He often brings presents home hoping to cheer her up. Sometimes his presents help, and sometimes not. He loves her dearly; making her happy has became his top priority. "Maybe if we had a child?" He would give it thought.

CHAPTER 20

Rebecca's business is more successful than she ever thought possible. She has prostitutes rotating from Baltimore, Philadelphia and Pittsburgh. She never has less than four working at a time and the clientele continues to be only successful businessmen. She is well known around town but doesn't worry; the townspeople respect her, they call her Miss Becky. The merchants are just as pleased to have her around. She is one of their best shoppers. She would think nothing of going into the jewelry store to spend a thousand dollars. Of course, she always paid in cash. Her girls had the best of everything available to them when they worked at her house. She bought expensive wigs, perfumes and the best clothing she could find. On holidays, Miss Becky furnished food baskets to poor families and bought little children warm coats and shoes. She walked down the street with her head held high and full of pride. Everyone greeted her.

As each prostitute rotated out, Miss Becky sent their clothing to the local dry cleaner, even the expensive bright-colored panties and bras. The dry cleaner would return the unmentionables neatly safety pinned to clothes hangers and they would hang in the closet awaiting the girls return. She kept the beauty shop busy, the cab company, the local florist, and even the local brewery. Rebecca's contribution to the community was impressive. Everyone liked her.

CHAPTER 21

Young school children, even though they didn't understand what prostitution was, would sit on second level porches, or third floor balconies, and watch the comings and goings of the affluent men. Sometimes they would recognize someone and report to their mother who they saw at Miss Becky's house. The well-to-do women, who had no need to rely on Miss Becky's donations, became furious and always called the police. Even though the chief of police and the judge, were regular customers to Miss Becky, they had to make the well-to-do woman happy and go through the arrest procedures. The judge's order would call for a very small fine with no disruption to business. Sometimes the arrest would make headlines, but names were never mentioned and this sold newspapers.

CHAPTER 22

When Marian gave birth to little John Ellis Jr., John was very careful to stay out of sight. When the doctor arrived for the delivery, John snuck out the back door. He could not allow the truth to be known. Marian later told John that the doctor made no comment. "It's a doctor's duty to keep his opinion to himself," John told Marian. John hoped the doctor would assume that this fair-skinned little boy was fathered while Marian was next door working for her sister.

Marian and John adored their "Little John" as they called him. But not allowing him to be seen in public with his father was heartbreaking to Marian. The townspeople whispered among themselves when they saw Marian with this beautiful, half-white little boy. "How could you expect me to expose myself to something like that?" John would ask her when she expressed her unhappiness to him. She knew the people wondered who the father was and she knew they thought this baby came from Miss Becky's house. The thought of her conceiving at Miss Becky's house made her sick to her stomach. John ask her, "If you think they gossip when they see him with you, imagine how it would be for me." The whole arrangement was beginning to affect Marian. She felt ridiculed when seen with her own son. Little John can't be seen in public with his own father, nor could they ever go out as a family. John was very affectionate to his son when he was home. Marian knows that John loves his son, so why does he admit to Marian that he is embarrassed to be seen in public with his own child? His feelings anger Marian. Now John is insisting that Little John will go to a private school somewhere out of town when he becomes of age. Marian is furious. As the baby grows, Marian is afraid to become attached. She knows at about the age of five, Little John will be taken away to attend private school. So now she pretends that she is just the housekeeper and it's her job to care for the baby while Daddy works. She pretends that preparing the meals and doing the shopping is just part of the job. Marian is becoming more and more angry at John with all his rules and concerns about saving himself from gossip.

CHAPTER 23

Miss Becky made headlines on three occasions within the last year. The one most disturbing to her was the article reporting the theft of twenty-seven thousand dollars, in cash, from the trunk in her house. The story was false. She did have money stashed in the trunk, but to her knowledge none had been stolen. She also had money hidden in the attic, under floorboards and in her mattress, just to name a few of her hiding places. She wondered how anybody would know about the money and decided to keep a closer watch on the prostitutes. The worst of it was that the headline brought on an Internal Revenue Service investigation, and she was forced to pay taxes in the amount of forty- two thousand dollars. The amount chosen was based on her estimated spending around town. Now that the news was out that she hid money in her house, she became the victim of attempted robbery six times in the next two years. Once while she and the girls were held at gunpoint, the burglars ransacked the house. But they never found all the hiding places. After finding one stash in the trunk, Rebecca assumed they thought they found it all, and they left in a hurry. The robberies resulted in problems convincing the prostitutes to stay. They didn't like the possibility of being killed over Miss Becky's money.

Miss Becky offered to pay her girls a higher percentage and promised she would protect them. She shared her ideas with them hoping to gain trust. Together, they decided that Rebecca should falsely report robberies to the police and claim just small amounts of money taken. "When the word gets out that there are no longer large amounts of money around here, the robberies will stop," Katherine said. Katherine had been working the house longer than anyone else, and Rebecca respected her opinion. Katherine also suggested to Rebecca that she use a bank from now on. Rebecca indicated she would. Now, even the girls think there is no cash worth taking. Rebecca felt safer. The police reports indicating that small amounts of money was stolen from Miss Becky always made the news, local reporters said that Miss Becky was now "banking her money,"and soon the robberies stopped.

CHAPTER 24

Now that Little John is in school someplace in Ohio, Marian is in a deep depression, and her anger against John has grown almost out of control. She fought with him every day; no matter how he tried to rationalize, he could not calm her down. John knew that sending Little John away was the reason for her state of mind, but he had a reputation to uphold and clientele to protect. He didn't feel he had any other choice. He missed Little John too but was determined to save himself from embarrassment. He was doing very well financially and simply had too much to lose. Marian had a difficult time with her depression and blamed it on John. One day when John came home from the office, Marian was waiting for him at the door. She had a can of kerosene in her hand; she threw it on him and lit a match. She sat on a nearby chair and watched him burn. A neighbor called the fire department and there were fire trucks everywhere. Too many fire trucks as far as Marian was concerned. She remained sitting in her chair and watched the firemen do their job. She felt no remorse.

When the police arrived to arrest Marian she said nothing. Rebecca heard the commotion next door, and for the first time in six years, she saw her sister. The newspaper reported that Attorney John Ellis was burned to death by his housekeeper. The trial was quick, the fireman reported their findings and Marian's state-appointed attorney offered no defense. Within hours she was found guilty by reason of insanity. She was sentenced indefinitely to the state mental institution where she was kept under heavy sedation. Little John was cared for through a trust fund arranged by his father.

Rebecca is very distraught by her sister's ill fate. She doesn't like the conditions Marian is subject to at the hospital and will see to it that one day Marian will come home. Rebecca will keep the house next door vacant and well-maintained. She's not sure if Marian will remember the fire, but she will make sure that all evidence is cleaned up. She is obsessed with the way the hospital is caring for Marian and believes that the heavy sedation is uncalled for. She will hire a lawyer and have him do everything possible to have Marian released from that awful place. Each time Rebecca visits, she becomes more disgusted. Marian lies on the bed in the nude in her own feces. Her meals are placed in front of her and most times not touched by Marian. The nurse comes to remove the tray without the slightest concern. It doesn't matter to the nurse if Marian eats her meals or not. She is so sedated that she isn't even aware that food had been placed in front of her. When Rebecca talked to the hospital administrator about her concerns and dissatisfaction with her sister's care, the administrator claimed that Marian chooses to stay in bed. "Bathing is only done on scheduled days," he said. When asked why Marian is nude, he again said: "That is Marian's choice." The medication was justified by the fact that Marian had killed someone, and murderers are sedated to protect the staff.

Rebecca told her attorney that Marian is sedated to the point that she doesn't even know who her sister is. "She doesn't know what she's doing, and yet the hospital says they allow her to make her own choices." Rebecca's attorney, William Jacobs, encouraged her to file charges against the hospital for the inhumane treatment of her sister.

Attorney Jacobs is a client at Miss Becky's, and so is the Judge. The hearing went smoothly. The judge ordered receipt of Marian's hospital records. Even though the legal authorities are working for their local madam, they still have to make all possible efforts to follow the law. Orders were properly prepared by Attorney Jacobs and appropriately signed with approval by the judge. Attorney Jacobs drove to the hospital with the signed court order and was immediately given Marian's records, a folder with no more than ten pages. According to the records, Marian has not yet been interviewed or examined by a doctor, even though she's been a patient for a little over six months. Her food intake has not been charted, nor treatment rendered for her bedsores. No record of bathing or changing her bed clothes. Nothing is mentioned about the extreme weight loss Marian has suffered or her lack of communication. It had been determined by the administrator that when Marian was admitted, she is to be considered dangerous and will be kept under heavy sedation. The document said that she was to be treated like the murderer that she is.

The judge was aware that treatment was limited to criminals who were sentenced to the State Hospital, but he was not aware that treatment was so inhumane. He occasionally has reason to sentence someone to the hospital for the criminally insane, like he had Marian, but he will think twice before doing it again. He ordered that Marian's medication be reduced by one half and that Miss Becky's attorney accompany her on future visits. The purpose of having the company of the attorney was to verify that Rebecca's statements about Marian's treatment were believed to be true. If this case should ever go before a jury, the judge wanted to be fully prepared. He ordered a full written report from Attorney Jacobs clearly stating his findings. The report is due in one month.

With the reduction of medication, Marian began showing some improvement but was not as responsive as Rebecca thought she should be. Rebecca knew that since "the accident," as Rebecca called it, Marian would probably never return to herself completely, but she expected more of a recovery than she was seeing. The judge ordered no medication for one month and ordered daily visits be allowed by Miss Becky and her attorney. He also ordered one staff person to be with Marian around the clock for the same month. He wanted daily written reports from hospital staff. The hospital administrator wasn't eager to comply, but he knew that a court order meant business. He had no other choice.

After Marian had been off the medication for the month, she began showing signs of returning to her normal behavior. Staff members reported that Marian was quiet and showed no signs of danger to herself or to others. Rebecca was elated and continued the daily visits until finally the judge ordered Marian's release. He made it clear, however, that Marian was to be under the custody of Miss Becky and that Miss Becky will be responsible for Marian's whereabouts at all times. He considered this to be the same as parole; after all, he said: "Marian did commit a crime."

Marian returned home to the house next door and went on about her business as though nothing had ever happened. Rebecca gave her money and Marian did her own shopping and cooking as usual. Marian was in good spirits when she was cooking or cleaning, but when the morning chores were done, she felt useless and depressed. Marian spent a good portion of her afternoons wandering the streets. She hung her head, walked slowly and never spoke to anybody. It appeared she was ashamed. Everyone around town knew who Marian was; they knew about her hospital stay, they even knew she was arrested for murder. But because she was the sister of the well-respected Miss Becky, they accepted her for who she was and tried not to stare.

Marian began to visit the merchants. She told unbelievable stories about not having anything to eat or heat in her house. She said her lights don't work and neither does her water. She started begging for food, clothes and newspapers. She said she needed the newspapers to keep warm. The merchants knew she was sick and that her stories were not true, but they attempted to take care of her as best they could. The merchants never mentioned a word to Miss Becky.

CHAPTER 25

In June of 1971, Miss Becky made major headlines. The Front cover said: IRS CHARGES MISS BECKY $75.000.00 IN UNPAID TAXES. The story said Miss Becky's house was robbed of large amounts of money. A prostitute reported the robbery to the police. She reported that she had been bound and gagged by a so-called client. She said she was working the afternoon shift and that Miss Becky had been out taking care of some business. The intruder entered the house posing as a client and accompanied one of the girls upstairs. When they entered the second floor, he pushed the girl into Miss Becky's room and immediately ordered her to lie on Miss Becky's bed. Then he tied her hands behind her back and put nylon stockings in her mouth. He pointed a gun at the prostitute's temple and told her if she made a sound he would shoot. He began ransacking the room and found a lot of money before he fled. The prostitute told the police officer that she had no idea how much money had been taken, but the sack he was carrying seemed to be full. Before the thief was out the door, one of the girls was on the phone to the police. "Thank God Miss Becky always kept the number for the police taped on the wall beside the phone," she said. The accused robber was picked up just a few blocks from Miss Becky's house within fifteen minutes after the robbery. The over- stuffed pillow case he was carrying was impossible for him to hide. His crammed pink silk sack stood out on the street and made him a easy catch for the police.

He had in his possession $103,000.00. When the police took the money to be held as evidence, the IRS was standing by to take their share.

Miss Becky closed the business for a few days. She allowed the girls who were present at the time of the robbery to leave and waited for a new rotation. In the weeks that followed the headlines, Miss Becky's business slowed down and she had fewer prostitutes willing to work for her. She had been through rough times before and knew that the down side would soon pass and business would return to normal. She believed the headlines and several follow-up stories were the main reason for the slump. But sometimes, she couldn't help but wonder if having Marian around discouraged the lawyers. She considered opening the house to a wider range of clients. She would allow merchant owners and sometimes even truck drivers, if they were clean. She would continue to turn the colored and the students away.

Miss Becky's establishment is now known nationwide. Allowing truck drivers to enter became her best source of advertizement. As word of mouth spread, truckers became her major source of income. She also had a few new girls that didn't quite meet her standards but they were reliable and clean. One, who Miss Becky called Babe, was a few pounds overweight, but it didn't seem to matter to her customers. Miss Becky soon discovered that some clients preferred a little weight. Babe became one of the most active prostitutes she ever had working for her. Babe was a bleached blond, lots of makeup and she appeared to be about thirty-five. She had a rough complexion and could use some of the foulest language Miss Becky had ever heard come from a woman's mouth. Miss Becky knew she gave the customer everything they ask for. Babe worked through her rotation and left to work in Pittsburgh. When she returned on rotation, she brought a friend with her who acted like and talked just as foul as Babe. Having just two girls, Babe and her friend, work for her, Miss Becky was making as much money as she had before when she had four full-time girls. Sometimes she still had four on rotation but since the latest news, Miss Becky knew she couldn't count on them. Most of the girls seemed to return only when they had no place else to go. Babe and her friend no longer rotated; they became very reliable and Miss Becky knew she could always count on them.

Miss Becky's house was robbed again, this time there were two robbers. One held Miss Becky and the girls at gunpoint while the other searched every corner of the house. They got away with somewhere around thirty thousand dollars. The robbers didn't find all the money; they didn't find all of Miss Becky's hiding places. Miss Becky didn't plan to report the theft; she didn't want the headlines again or be forced to report to the Internal Revenue Service. But Babe was very shaken and called the police. The neighbors were upset about the constant flow of police cars on their block. The sirens and red flashing lights often woke them and their children during the night. They constantly complained about the legality of the establishment in their neighborhood. Miss Becky had lost the police chief as a client, and so the police department started to follow up on every complaint they received. Since lawyers rarely cater to her business any longer and since she also lost the judge as her client, the law no longer ignored the illegal operation. Miss Becky blamed her bad luck on the unfair adverse publicity. The robbery again made headlines. Miss Becky was charged with illegal solicitation, ordered to close the business and to spend one night in jail. She was charged with a steep fine. Miss Becky paid the fine, spent the night in jail, but did not close her business.

Miss Becky continued to give to the poor, but she wasn't the shopper she used to be. She is older now, guessed to be in her seventies, and has difficulty walking. Her passion for ice cream has added many pounds to her small frame. She had eaten so much over the years that now her obesity is interfering with her daily living habits. Recently the strain is showing and she has become unattractive. Other than obesity, she is a healthy woman. Most times, she sends one of the girls out to do the shopping. She makes weekly arrangements by phone with the grocer to deliver to any family he thought was in need. Her lack of presence on the streets is noticed and she decided that might be another reason for all the complaints. In the past everyone liked her. When she walked the street, everyone spoke to her. Now that she is no longer visible, she wonders if the people miss her, "or do they think I have something to hide?" She is aware that Marian spends most of her time walking around town and wonders if Marian is spreading rumors.

Three a.m., June 17, 1972. The police were again called to Miss Becky's house. The prostitute calling said she found Miss Becky murdered in her bed. She had been stabbed to death. After the coroner pronounced Miss Becky dead, the body was removed from the house. Because the police found no money, they quickly determined the motive for the murder was robbery. Miss Becky had been stabbed only one time in the chest with a large sharp object. The one deep stab proved to be all that was needed to kill the victim. The police couldn't find a murder weapon, any signs of struggle or forced entry. The murder made national news, and several tabloids. Some reported hundreds of thousands of dollars stole from the "madam's" house. Some even speculated about who they thought had murdered Miss Becky. The investigation went on for months. The police had no clues. They interrogated the prostitutes, spent extra time with the girl who had reported the murder and could not come up with a single explanation. They questioned local merchants and even talked to Marian, who of course, made no sense when she answered the questions.

CHAPTER 26

The longer Marian is next door, the more angry she becomes. She doesn't feel sadness about her dead sister; she continues to hold a grudge against Rebecca and can't forget that she operated that awful business. She thinks that Rebecca and her awful business is responsible for John coming to her in the first place. Because of John, she produced a half-breed baby, and because of John, the boy was taken away from her, and because of John, she was sent to the State Hospital. Sometimes, when she connects with John in a seance, she reminds him of all the horrible things he has done to her. She accuses him of causing her illness and criticizes him for patronizing the house next door. She curses him for coming to her only after he was turned down from Miss Becky's. She loathes him when he refuses to tell her where Little John is.

Marian hasn't forgotten that she didn't approve of Rebecca's establishment. And she hasn't forgotten her son. She knows he is in Ohio and she often phones the information operator asking for Little John's telephone number. She has considered asking the merchants for money so she could catch a bus to Ohio and search the streets for him.

Two years after Miss Becky's murder, the police still haven't solved the crime. They searched the property numerous times and found no evidence. They decided to release the crime scene and remove the orange tape that had encircled the area for the past two years. Once the tape was removed and the house had been abandoned by the police, Marian thought it would be better for her if she moved into Rebecca's house. She remembered how John died, how she watched him burn and she still smells that disgusting odor each time she enters her door. She isn't sorry she did it and she's glad Rebecca is gone too. Rebecca's clothes are still in the house next door, and sometimes Marian likes to get all dressed up. She remembers the fancy jewelry and the wigs. Maybe if there are still high-heeled shoes, she might try those too.

It's been two years since the utilities have been disconnected in both properties. It didn't matter to Marian, she never used them anyway. Furthermore, Marian didn't know enough to pay the bills; even if she did, she had no money. She relied on the merchants to provide her with the bare necessities. She found food in garbage cans behind restaurants and sometimes found a whole meal waiting for her at the back door of one particular diner. She found a piece of scrap tin, placed it in the middle of the living room floor, put newspaper on top and set the paper on fire. She used the indoor fire for light and to keep herself warm. She always wore Miss Becky's clothes and usually looked nice when she went out. She flaunts the expensive jewelry, and on occasion becomes a blond in high heels.

CHAPTER 27

It's been more than one hundred years since Mary Elizabeth first arrived in Pennsylvania. Over the years, the small town has grown to a population of almost twenty-two thousand residences. Saturday morning market no longer takes place at the four corners. The Farmer's Market, as it is now called, has moved to a large building at the east end of town and is open Thursday, Friday and Saturday. The market has a sit-down restaurant, indoor bathrooms and approximately fifty vendors. Local farmers still bring their fruits and vegetables, but now they have the convenience of refrigeration. Items such as milk and fresh meats are also available. Each space is rented to the farmer and they are supplied with lighted meat counters and fancy tables to display their crafts and homemade baked goods.

The second courthouse has been built on the four corners, the streets are paved and now drivers have the inconvenience of four-way stop signs and red lights. The law school built a new football field and a large athletic center. Law students keep the many new restaurants and bars in business.

A new shopping center has been built at the south end of town and shoppers are going to the shopping center instead of downtown to do their shopping. Family owned businesses that have been handed down through generations are facing serious economic problems. Local merchants have formed a Merchant's Association to discuss possible solutions. Association representatives attend meetings with town council regularly to express their concerns.

The shopping center had a huge grocery store which is its main attraction. Shoppers can purchase shoes, clothing, drugs, furniture and even do their banking all under the same roof. A large parking lot was provided; shoppers didn't have to travel for blocks to find parking and they didn't have to pay parking meters. Town council and the merchants agreed that if parking were made more convenient, shoppers might return to the downtown area to do their shopping.

When town council learned that the state is advertizing the availability of federal funds to be used for revitalization of small towns in Pennsylvania, town council met with the leaders of the other surrounding communities explaining the details of the grant. The funds available are to be shared county-wide and not to be used solely by any one particular town. Town council thought that if they had the support of the other communities, they would apply for the funds and offer to man the project locally for county distribution. Some of the communities did not meet the population criteria, and therefore would not benefit from the funds.

Town council applied for the grant and within a year, the funds were approved. First priority was for the revitalization of the county seat. They will use the government funds to improve parking in the downtown area and hopefully encourage the shoppers to return. They hired a consulting firm to provide studies and make suggestions on how to bring business back to the downtown area. They asked for drawings on proposals for new sidewalks, street lights and to make recommendations for additional parking lots. They ask for "face lift" guidance on improving a four-square-block area.

After the consultant firm came back with acceptable drawings for the revitalization, the council put into use the budgeted funds available for administration of the program. They opened a new office and hired a director and one clerical clerk.

As the new director studied the plans, he found only one area that would require demolition to make room for one of the new proposed parking lots. The proposal required demolition of two residential properties, Marian's house and the house next door, Miss Becky's house. The two properties were very run-down and, if occupied, the program would offer relocation. Utility records indicated that services were disconnected soon after the death of the owner, giving the assumption that the two houses were vacant.

The director, Raymond (Ray) E. Wentz, visited the properties in order to study the necessary requirements needed in preparation for demolition. There were no keys available for him to enter the houses, but his exterior inspection indicated that the properties would be easy to take down. But first the manifestation of rodents would have to be exterminated as the first step in preparing the properties. Ray found evidence of serious rat infestation. He would have to exterminate all the surrounding properties so the rodents couldn't run from these two buildings and invade neighboring houses. Knowing the history of the property, Ray was curious; he decided to return with a hammer, a crowbar or whatever it took for him to get inside.

Upon his return to Miss Becky's house, hammer in hand, he was met at the door by a very elderly black women. She began yelling and telling him to go away. "Nobody is here," she said. He tried talking to her, but she immediately went into the house and slammed the door almost literally in his face. He was stunned. He was told that both properties were vacant. He would have to do some research and report to the council that demolition would have to be postponed until he was sure that the house was not permanently occupied. Ray spoke with merchants to ask about the woman. They knew exactly who he was talking about. They said she was Miss Becky's sister; she was crazy and told stories about how she cleaned for the colonel. She told stories about how she scrubbed the colonel's cellar from top to bottom. She told them she talks to the dead and that she claims that someone keeps stealing her legacy. Ray was at a loss; he wasn't sure what he needed to do next.

After the program solicitor examined courthouse records, he discovered that one of the houses, he didn't know which one, had been deeded to Marian Thompson back in the 1930's. The assumption that both houses belonged to the deceased, Rebecca Thompson, was incorrectly assumed. He told Ray that he would have to go through the eminent domain process to eventually obtain legal entry to the house. "If Marian wants to slam the door in your face, at this point, she had every right to do so," he said. And so, the long procedure necessary to acquire the property legally has begun.

In the meantime, Ray asked his clerical clerk if she would mind checking in on Marian. "Perhaps a women can talk to her," he said. The clerk, an outgoing person in her late twenties, is married and has two small children. Her name is Janice Collins.

Now that Janice's two children have started attending school, she thought that she might like to work outside the home. She had never had a job before but she did know how to type (slowly). She hoped knowing how to type was enough to qualify her for the job. What impressed Ray so much during his employment interview with her was her ability to defend herself for not having prior work experience. Janice told Ray that her past work record included experience with duties such as budgeting, nursing, physiology and transportation. She was responsible for educating, planning, and also served as a nutritionist to her family. Janice insisted that parenting and operating a household successfully should definitely be considered as notable experience. After listing to her imagination, how could he turn her down? He liked her and he hired her on the spot. She was fun to work with and he knew that she was more capable than anyone to get through to Marian. He hoped that her experience in physiology would pay off.

CHAPTER 28

Janice was excited to have the opportunity to become involved in such an historical event that took place in her own hometown. She remembered the headlines she had read about Miss Becky and the stories she had heard about Miss Becky's sister, Marian. She was anxious to meet this person, Marian. Her first visit was not very successful. Marian wouldn't answer the door.

The next day Janice knocked on Marian's door. Marian opened the door, just a few inches, and in a loud voice said, "I'm not hiring, go away."

Janice laughed when she told Ray about the experience. "She thought I was a prostitute looking for a job." It took a few weeks of daily visits for Janice to get Marian to open the door, or to get more than three or four words from her. On occasion, Marian would talk about things Janice never head of. On one particular day, Marian told Janice that she couldn't come in because the colonel was visiting. Eventually Janice learned to go along with Marian's imagination and participate in any subject Marian wanted to talk about. So next time, when Marian said the colonel was visiting, Janice said, "Oh good, tell him I said hello."

Marian turned her head away from the door, as if she was talking to someone behind her, and yelled: "Janice says hello, Colonel."

On one of Janice's visits, Marian claimed to be holding a seance. She opened the door only a few inches, just far enough for Janice to see that Marian had sprinkled her whole body, from head to toe, with something that looked like white powder or flour. Marian was angry at Janice for interrupting her seance. "Interruptions could cause me to lose contact with my visitor, and I may never be able to reach him again. Now you go away. I told you last time you were here that I wasn't hiring." Janice didn't know what to say to Marian so she left the porch immediately. For the first time, Janice felt afraid of Marian.

After telling Ray the story, he told Janice to stay away for a few days. He said he had a new project for her anyway. He wanted her to go to the Social Security Office and see if she could arrange benefits for Marian. Janice was eager to do anything to help. It never entered her mind that Marian had no money. The Social Security Office was directly across the street. Janice could see it from her desk. She finished up some odds and ends on her desk and within the hour she was across the street. She explained to the receptionist who she was and why she had come. The receptionist said: "Sorry we can't help. We need birth certificates, the applicant's signature and proof of citizenship." Janice asked the receptionist how she could go about getting a birth certificate. "From the Vital Statistics Office in Washington DC," she rudely answered. Janice ask if this office could do the request for her. She was rudely told, "No."

By this time, Janice was getting a little angry at the reception she was receiving. She folded her arms across her chest and took a seat in the reception area. She looked at the person behind the desk and decided that anyone that nasty must really hate her job. Janice got up from the chair, unfolded her arms, and walked up to the mean lady and clearly said: "I know you can help me, but I don't think you want to, so I will just stay here until I get what I came after." She returned to her chair, refolded her arms and stared down the receptionist. At five o'clock when the Social Security Office closed for the day, the receptionist and Janice went home. But at eight o'clock the next morning, Janice returned to her waiting spot. Soon a woman who appeared to have more authority than the receptionist came up to Janice and asked her to follow her to her desk. The lady said: "Sandy, the receptionist, told me why you were here yesterday and I decided to take on the challenge myself. Sandy doesn't have to know; she is only doing her job."

The woman, who never identified herself, said she already checked with vital statistics and there is no record of Marian's birth. "But that doesn't mean we can't help; it's our duty to provide for people like Marian." She told Janice: "I know who Marian is, I've seen her around town. It would be helpful if you could return with someone who would be willing to take responsibility for Marian's monthly allotment, should it be approved. The payment check would have to be direct deposit, probably to a local bank. This person should agree to set up a trust fund for Marian." The next day Janice returned to the Social Security Office with a member of town council, who happens to also be a banker. Together the banker and the women organized the details. Marian would begin receiving benefits within ninety days.

Janice waited until the end of the ninety days to tell Marian about the Social Security payment. She explained to Marian that she would have go to the bank to get her spending money. "Every Thursday, Marian, you go to the bank. Anyone who works there will know that you have come for your money."

Marian said: "It's about time they stop stealing my legacy." During the conversation, Janice noticed that Marian kept looking over her shoulder at the loading dock across the street. It was the shipping and receiving area for a local furniture store. Marian said to Janice: "You see that truck? It's full of

Confederate soldiers, they have come to steal from me. They always take my legacy from my mailbox."

The truck belonged to the Mason Dixon Trucking Company. On the trailer was a life-sized painted logo of two uniformed Civil War soldiers, one representing the north and the other representing the south. Marian said: "Soldiers hide in that truck and any chance they get, they come over here and steal my legacy. They've been doing it for fifty years."

When Janice tried to explain to Marian that she would have to move soon, Marian pretended like she never heard a word Janice was saying. When Janice attempted to get Marian to look at a few houses and choose one she liked, explaining that the project would purchase it for her, she refused to acknowledge that she understood the conversation. Janice told Ray that it's time to get serious with Marian. "I've been visiting that old woman for more than a year now and she keeps making excuses every time I try to tell her why I come visiting." The program couldn't wait any longer for Marian to cooperate. They had deadlines to meet according to the terms of the grant, and so they were forced to made a relocation purchase without Marian's approval. The property was only a block away from where Marian now lives. The house had hot and cold running water, electricity and even a working bathroom. It was completely furnished including kitchen appliances, curtains on the windows and carpeting on the floors. The program paid the full purchase price for the house, so there was no mortgage for Marian. The banker will take care of the utility bills and budget for her weekly allowance. "If only Marian were capable of realizing how much better things will be for her," Janice told Ray.

Janice started talking to Marian about her rundown house and told her straightforward that the town had bought it and paid the money to her legacy at the bank. Janice also told Marian that soon, within a few weeks, the town was going to tear down her house to make room for a new parking lot. Marian made no comment, and at first Janice thought that maybe she didn't comprehend. Janice said in clear, plain English, "Marian, you are going to have to move to another house."

Marian looked directly into Janice's eyes and said "I have to ask the colonel if it will be alright."

Days and weeks passed. The conversation of the new house came up with each visit. Marian never responded. Finally, Janice ask Marian if she would like to go down the street to see her new house. She explained to Marian that probably the colonel would like to know where it is. "When you move there, Marian, the colonel will have to know where you live so he can find you when he wants to come visit." Marian agreed to see the new house. They walked the block, entered the house and Janice gave Marian the tour. The walk-through was very complete. Janice felt like a realtor trying to impress a buyer for a potential real estate transaction. Janice turned on the appliances, flushed the toilet and ran water from each faucet. She even offered Marian a drink of water with a glass taken from the fully-furnished kitchen cabinets. Marian said nothing, showed no expression and walked out of the house with Janice at her footsteps. They walked back to Marian's without a word spoken.

Janice reported her adventure to Ray; he, in turn, reported to town council. Council was getting very upset that this silly old lady was capable of manipulating the council and interfering with town progress. The spokesman told Ray that "demolition will be scheduled for three weeks from today. The old lady has a place to go, and might I add a much better place than she has ever had." He said: "I will direct the maintenance crew to board the place up today. Fire regulations require that only one means of entry and exit must be kept accessible. We will board all the windows and doors. We will keep the back door open for access. The house will become very dark and so cold that Marian will be begging us to take her to her new house."

When Janice visited the next day, every window and the front door was boarded shut. She had to go around to the back and knock on Marian's back door. This was a bit spooky for Janice. She had never been behind the house before. The back stoop was covered with overgrown bushes and had some kind of sticky buildup, a few inches thick, of some ugly, almost black in color substance. The concrete and the soil around the small porch was just covered with this stuff. Whatever it is, it has a very bad, wicked odor and it is sticking to Janice's shoes.

Just as Janice arrived, Marian was coming out the back door and ready to walk downtown. Janice noticed Marian's dress was open in the back from the hem to the waist. It looked as if it had been cut. Marian was not wearing underwear. Janice told her to go in and change. "Marian you can't go downtown showing your bare butt, people might laugh." Marian was in an agreeable mood today and did as she was told. When she came back from changing her dress, Janice noticed that Marian had done something to increase the size of her breasts. They were huge. When she walked they wiggled. Janice hoped she wasn't losing her mind, but she thought she heard strange noises coming from Marian's breasts. Janice asked Marian: "Where did you get those big boobs?" Marian proceeded to unbutton her dress and show Janice her trick. She had put a rope around her neck, and at both ends, she had attached two plastic bags filled with water. The two bags of water were hanging at her chest. Janice told Marian that her boobs made funny noises and that people would probably hear her coming. She told Marian that they didn't look real. "They gurgle too much." Marian ignored her and walked away. She headed downtown.

Janice called to Marian: "Three weeks, Marian, and you have to move to the new house."

Another time when Janice went to see Marian, Marian was in a very angry mood. She quickly opened the door and plunged toward Janice with her arm raised and a knife in her hand. Janice grabbed her wrist, and while holding Marian's arm up in the air, yelled at her, "Marian don't you ever do that to me again; I will tell the colonel." Marian relaxed her arm, threw the knife to the side yard, turned around and slammed the door. Janice yelled: "Two more weeks, Marian, and you will have to move to the new house."

Janice knew that Marian was angry with her. Most visits resulted in some kind of nasty words or actions from Marian. Visits always ended with Marian slamming the door and Janice yelling: "twelve more days, ten more days, eight more days."

During the last week that Marian was to remain in her house, Janice went to visit and was met at the door with a bucket of sticky, foul smelling, almost liquid substance being thrown out at her. With that shocking greeting, Janice was so furious, and without even thinking, went storming into the house after Marian. This is the first time Janice has ever been inside Marian's house. When she entered the almost dark house and rushed into the front parlor in a fury, she saw Marion casually standing there, gawking like she was surprised to have company. Janice was so angry, she just stared at Marian in disbelief. They both stood, staring at the other, neither with anything to say. Janice finally regained her composure and stopped staring. She looked around the room and curiosity studied the collection of small buckets, coffee cans and large jars lined up evenly along every wall in the room. "What is all this, Marian?" she said while pointing to the arrangement.

Marian proceeded to explain to Janice that she uses the

containers to go to the bathroom. When they are all full, she sprinkles salt on top, pours everything into a large bucket and throws it out the back door. "That's how I get rid of the evil spirits," she told Janice. Enough of what the stuff is on the back porch, Janice thought. She turned around, ran out the door and vomited on the sidewalk. She returned to her office long enough to pick up her car keys, and then went home to shower.

The next day, Friday, Janice reluctantly went to Marian's for what she hoped to be the last time. The moving truck was scheduled to come tomorrow, Saturday. She was greeted quietly. She talked slowly and directly to Marian. She was tired of being messed around with by this old lady and wanted Marian to understand that tomorrow, at eight a.m., the truck would be here to take her belongings to the new house. Janice explained to Marian that she will be here to help and if Marian wanted her to, she would go to the new house with her. Marian, in her quiet mood, said: "I can't go unless the colonel tells me it's alright."

Janice raised her voice. "Did you ever ask the colonel, Marian?"

Marian instantly showed anger. She began yelling about Miss Becky and her business, and all the corruption that has taken place in this house. She talked about the robberies; she said more than once that she used to be scared. She kept repeating in a very angry voice: "I told Rebecca that prostitution was wrong, wrong, wrong." Her voice got louder each time she said the word wrong. She said: "I told Rebecca that prostitution was evil and would end in death." She said: "I told Rebecca that if she didn't stop performing evil acts in this house I would have to kill her, and I did." Janice quickly decided not to say anything about this conversation to anyone. Not yet anyway. She knew that Rebecca's murder had never been solved. She had to sort her thoughts; is Marian telling the truth or is she just imagining?

Saturday morning, when the truck arrived, Marian was nowhere to be found. The men proceeded to take the boards from the front door; they searched the house to be sure it was vacant, then began removing Marian's personal belongings. They all had interesting comments to make to each other. One worker asked the other: "Did you see the dried up chocolate ice cream stains on the front of the refrigerator? It looks like it has been there for a hundred years."

Another said, "I can't wait to tell my wife I spent the morning at Miss Becky's house." There must have been ten dead rats found in dresser drawers, kitchen cabinets and in the basement. Most noticeable to Janice was the large butcher knife found in the kitchen in the trash can. Janice worked quietly helping to carry Marian's and Rebecca's belongings to the truck, but had very little to say. She was worried about Marian's comments from yesterday and wondered where Marian was now. Janice decided that she would have to remain in the area until she saw Marian coming back to the house. She was curious about Marian's reaction when she returned and discovered that she couldn't get into the house. All the doors would be boarded after the house was vacant. Janice had to be sure that Marian would have a place to sleep tonight.

The personal belongings are gone, the truck is gone and the house is completely boarded up again. It is locked up so tight that Janice thought even a mouse couldn't get in. Janice remained in the area, stayed out of sight, and was determined to wait for Marian's return. It wasn't long until Marian walked up on the front porch, stared at the nails and the boards, walked around to the back of the house and studied the situation even longer. She had finally given in. As Janice followed, she watched

Marian walk down the street for only one block, and enter the unlocked front door of her new house. The daily visits were finally over. She would miss Marian but she would not miss the daily challenge of having to deal with the unexpected. Hopefully, Marian likes her new home. With relief Janice went home to be with her family.

CHAPTER 29

Three months have passed since Janice quit her job. It took three years to relocate Marian and enough was enough. Janice often thought about Marian and occasionally drove by her new house to see how things looked. Nothing has changed, except now, the curtains are always drawn shut. Janice decided that Marian liked to live in the dark. Darkness creates a perfect atmosphere for a seance, or secret visits from the colonel, she chuckled to herself. She hoped to catch a glance of Marian, either around her house or someplace on the street. She even thought of stopping to visit someday. But they were just thoughts and she never saw her again. She has not forgotten that Marian insinuated that she murdered Rebecca. Janice kept the secret to herself. She decided that no one needed to know and felt comfortable with her decision. Marian acted crazy, but Janice knew she was smarter than anybody would ever realize.

The two properties are now demolished, and in their place is a brand new parking lot. The new lot is so small that somehow moving the old women from her home didn't seem worthwhile. Janice wondered if Marian recognized the area. Or what she was doing while the demolition was taking place. "I bet she didn't miss a trick," Janice said to herself.

Headlines: MARIAN THOMPSON BURNS HOUSE DOWN. Janice couldn't believe what she was reading. It was reported that Marian must have run out of luck. Her habit of heating her house with tin and newspapers finally caught up with her. Marian was uninjured and relocated to a large, nearby, rundown, one-room apartment. Janice couldn't ignore her desire to see Marian. "I'm inquisitive, I want to see her just one more time." Janice went to visit Marian in the apartment. After the visit she was sorry she went. The building was rundown to the point of near condemnation. The interior hallways were covered with graffiti, the other tenants sat around in the halls among months worth of trash, smoking cigarettes and drinking beer. The place was very scary to Janice. She took the creepy, rattling, outdated elevator to the fifth floor where she was told Marian lived. As she walked down the hall, she saw and smelled the disgusting evidence of Marian's ritual, the one she used to chase the evil spirits away. Janice knew she was at the right place. Surprisingly, after just a light knock, Marian opened the door, asked Janice for a cigarette, which Janice was prepared to offer, and allowed Janice to come in. There was a single bed and a toilet in the room. No other conveniences. Janice couldn't believe that town council agreed to let Marian to live like this. There was very little conversation between them. If Marian remembered Janice, she pretended not to. Janice didn't stay long. That same night she dreamed about the roaches she saw on Marian's bed. Janice wondered who had the privilege of moving Marian into that god-awful place. Marian lived there for the next three years.

At the age of eighty-nine, Marian continued to wonder the streets. She no longer had Rebecca's clothes or fancy jewelry, her appearance was that of a very dirty, unkept homeless person. She walked wherever she wanted; to her, it didn't matter if she was fully clothed or not. She often yelled at strangers. She called them names and accused them of stealing from her. County commissioners decided that they have had enough of this crazy woman wondering the streets in their town and took it upon themselves to relocate Marian again. This time, they sent her to the county nursing home, where she died at the age of ninety-one.

* * * * *